How to Get Over Your Ex:

A Step By Step Guide to Mend a Broken Heart—Italian American Style

Rachel Russo

ISBN 978-1-62646-962-4

Published by BookLocker.com, Inc., Bradenton, Florida.

Printed in the United States of America.

BookLocker.com, Inc.
2014

First Edition

Dedication

This book is dedicated to all my paisanos who just want to love, be loved in return, and enjoy a nice bowl of spaghetti.

CONTENTS

Acknowledgements .... **IX**

Disclaimer .... **XI**

Introduction: Ciao Bella & Bello .... **XIII**

Been there, Done that XV
The Rx for Heartbreak-- Italian American Style XVI
Baby Steps in Your Quest to Get Over Your Ex XIX

Step 1: Forgetaboutit: Realize Your Relationship Just Got Whacked **1**

The Grief Phase--Italian American Style 3
Forgetaboutit! 6
Action Steps To Help You Realize Your Relationship Just Got Whacked . 10
Get rid of the evidence. *10*
Stai Zitto: Enforce a strict no contact policy. *11*
Get real through the written word. *12*

Step 2: Flip Tables & Cry: Get Mad & Sad--Because You Are Too Good For This **13**

Action Steps To Get Mad, Sad, And Realize You Are Too Good For This 22
Go to a bookstore and walk out empowered. *22*
Make a list of all the reasons why your ex is a stunad. *22*
Evaluate your ex by considering some common stunad red flags. *23*
Here are some signs of a stunad male ex: 23
Here are the signs of a stunad female: 25

Step 3: Make A Case For Stubbornness: Have A Head Like A Rock **29**

Two Types of People in The World 29
You Don't Need That Shit 32
Holiday Survival Tips 33
Fantasy vs. Reality 35
Action Steps to Make a Case for Stubbornness and Have a Head Like a Rock 39
Recognize all of your strengths and take pride in them. *39*
Get in touch with your stubborn side. *39*
Always remind yourself why you should get over your ex. *39*

Step 4: Stay Up & Fight-- For A Healthy (Single)Life 41
Single & Loving It 44
The Ex Encounter: Because You Can't Always Live In An Ex-Free Zone 46
Action Steps to Stay Up and Fight for a Healthy Single Lifestyle 50
Take care of your physical health. 50
Take care of your mental health. 51
Take care of your emotional health. 51

Step 5: Have Sunday Dinner: Family, Friends, & Food 53
Actions Steps To Have Sunday Dinner: Enjoy Family, Friends, And Food 64
Confide in your family and friends. 64
Ask for honest feedback. 64
Eat well. 65
Nutella Bouchee - Brownies 65

Step 6: La Dolce Vita: Live The Good Life 67
Create a unique personal style that is true to who you are 76
Keep it classy, biatches 77
Make sure everything is flattering 77
Groom with greatness 77
Mind your manners 78
Think carefully about what you say and how you say it 78
Catch'em with confidence 79
Action Steps to Live La Dolce Vita 80
Take inventory of your image, and make improvements where you need to. 80
Make over your bedroom and suitcase. 80

Step 7: Attract a Better Match: How to Find Amore or Something Like It 85
Exorcizing Your Ex 90
The Truth, The Whole Truth, And Nothing But The Truth 91
Meeting Other Singles 95
Action Steps You Should Take To Attract Amore Or Something Like It 106
Make a Wish List. 106

Let your old relationship rest in peace. *108*
Remember: Put yourself out there in a place where you can meet other singles. Just do it. *109*

Getting In The Last Word: Badda Bing, Badda Boom 111

Acknowledgements

The creation of this book owes its existence to many people. I would especially like to thank my parents, Robin and Alphonse Russo, who not only made and raised me Italian American, but encouraged my reading and writing abilities from childhood; all my favorite English teachers who nurtured my talent along the way; FabJob Inc. for publishing my first book, *A FabJob Guide to Become a Matchmaker,* and giving me the skills and courage to write a second; Shelli Trung, for choosing me as Ms. New York of 3six5dates.com and showing me how to turn my life experiences into great content; my editor, Rachel Sokol for her professionalism, wisdom, and humor; my "Eyetalian" American friend, Dan Perrone, for adding his two cents; every single person who has given me an opportunity that shaped my career in the matchmaking, dating, and relationship coaching industry; as well as all the friends, family, and fans who have graced me with the kind words and support that encourages me to keep going on my unique career path. Many thanks to God for never giving me a sensible 9-5p.m. with health insurance and a 401K. (Sorry, Dad.)

I would also like to express my deepest gratitude to all of my clients who have shared their stories and trusted me with the privilege of helping them in such a personal, important part of their lives. My work with both singles and couples has taught me more about myself and life in general than I could have ever imagined.

Interestingly enough, I am thankful for every guy who has ever broken my heart in even the slightest way. So here's to the boys who have unconsciously inspired me to become the better, stronger, and more loving version of myself. Without them, I would have never known that I am not only strong enough to heal my own heart, but that I can heal others hearts too!

I will never stop appreciating those who helped me along in my own heart-mending journey. I'd like to thank each and every one of my family members and friends for their support during the times when I needed to learn how to leave the past in the past.

Special thanks to those who have participated the most in this journey including my mother, Robin Russo, my sister, Chrissy Russo-Merxhushi, my Aunt Julie Nidle, my dear friend, Seph Dietlin, my cousin, Allison Russo, and my long-time girlies Rosalba Bambara, Georgina Tafaro, Lindsay Coronato, Daniela Baglieri, and Nicole Maiello, for listening to more than their fair share of relationship drama and kindly offering their perspective. My friends Sammy Lesman and Craig Bersen get a shout out for their patience too! Also, thanks to Angelina Kuhn for being a great friend and partner in crime on the Girls Nights Out/Man Hunts that proved to be an excellent distraction and my friend Jennifer West for always making me laugh.

Lastly, thanks to my Aunt Catherine Lembo for being the strong, independent woman who reminds me why I should never put up with a strunz!

If I didn't have such caring people in my life, I would not be where I am today. Trust me, the only thing harder than mending a broken heart is trying to mend your broken heart and publish a self-help breakup book while you are doing it!

But books, like relationships, are meant to be finished when they are meant to be finished.

Now, let's get to the mending, shall we?

Disclaimer

Thank you for purchasing *How to Get Over Your Ex: A Step by Step Guide to Mend a Broken Heart—Italian American Style!* No exes were harmed in the making of this book, which is a resource for educational and informational purposes. In my writing, I've used my personal and professional experiences, the experiences of friends, and various other sources, to provide you with sound advice for recovering from the aftermath of a breakup. That being said, my advice is opinion-based and is taken into account at your own risk.

Let's be honest: Finding, keeping, or ending love is a risky business. Unfortunately, like most things in life, my advice doesn't come with any guarantees, as there are subjective factors that are not within my control. If you need personalized relationship advice, you should hire a dating and relationship coach (hint, hint) or a licensed therapist. As you'll soon find out, I'm an expert at what I do, have serious credentials, and letters after my name to prove it. However, I should probably mention that I am not a licensed psychologist, and this book does not replace the care of such a mental health care professional.

My depiction of Italian Americans is based on my interpretation of the culture as an Italian American who grew up in Northern New Jersey, came of age in the early twenty-first century, and has spent several years living in my current home, NYC. It is not my intent to generalize or perpetuate any negative stereotypes about Italians or Americans of Italian descent or to offend anyone of any race, religion, gender, sexual orientation, or ethnicity. You do not need to be Italian American to appreciate and apply the advice in this book. You don't even have to like spaghetti! *But, seriously, what kind of person doesn't like spaghetti?* Contrary to popular belief, Italian Americans don't always do it better, and there are other cultures that have similar core values and successes. Still, the Italian Americans are pretty damn awesome and have a way of life that can truly help you get over your ex. Be warned: If you aren't Italian American, this book-which is one part self-help and one part celebration of Italian American culture-might just make you want to be!

Introduction:

Ciao Bella & Bello

Italian Americans are warm and welcoming people, but generally not as welcoming as "real" Italians; so I'll keep this introduction brief.

Having a broken heart sucks.

Naturally, after a painful breakup, most people are looking to cure their broken heart. I say forget the cure and just strive to mend your heart instead--Italian American style.

Who am I?

Well, I used to be a broken hearted girl. I mean a sad-tissue-hogging-chocolate-eating-venting-to-my-friends-daily-closure-seeking-kind-of-girl. I was hoping for a happy, healthy, sustainable relationship, but instead found myself single in the big city--going on ninety-two dates in one year and writing about them as Ms. New York of the international reality dating blog, 3six5dates.com, to be exact.

Additionally, I am a well-respected dating and relationship expert, therefore, I agreed to embark upon this reality-date-a-thon-in the name of social research. To be clear, I was not just the self-proclaimed kind of "expert" who has read every book in the self-help section of Barnes & Noble--though I could add that to my list of credentials. While we are on the subject, I have a master's degree in Marriage & Family Therapy, a bachelor's degree in psychology, a certification as an Intentional Relationship Coach, and nine years of experience working as a Matchmaker and Dating, Relationship, & Image Coach. *Did I mention I got a client married by ghostwriting his online dating profile and messages?* I figured if this social research experiment didn't result in my finding my own Mr. Right, my time in the dating trenches could at least help me better assist my clients--not to mention improve my writing, get me some press, and make me the most fascinating person in the room at dinner parties!

The clients I had helped establish successful relationships included everyone from college students, to CEOs of Fortune 500 companies, to NFL players, to retired senior citizens. They all had at least two things in common: They benefited from my advice on matters of the heart and appreciated my willingness to share my first-hand dating and relationship experience. The word on the street was that I had proven myself to be excellent at helping diverse people find and keep love. I had experienced a lot of personal satisfaction through my work and was always grateful for a career that let me make a difference in peoples' lives.

But soon after I finished my gig as Ms. New York, I realized I wanted to do even more to help the individuals who needed it most. Who were the people that were up at 2 a.m. struggling to make sense of their love life? The brokenhearted, of course.

You see throughout my gig as a serial dater, I learned that everything my clients were saying was true: Dating in NYC was no walk in the park. Serial dating in NYC while simultaneously trying to get over an ex? Even harder! (There's just something about a bad date that makes a girl want to run back into the familiar arms of even the worst of exes.) In retrospect, I discovered that serial dating wasn't the heartbreak cure. *It is not that I really thought it would be; but, hey, you never know!*

When I realized that even ninety-two dates didn't help me get over my ex, I wondered what would. Should I move to a city with a more favorable male to female ratio? *Nah, dating outside of the Big Apple would have its own challenges. Plus, it'd be really hard to live in a place where everything I could ever want was not just at my fingertips.* Was there something specific I could I do to move forward? Could I discover a way to let go of the past and be confident that there's someone else better for my future even when Mr. Right was nowhere in sight? Could I come up with a strategy for getting over an ex that I could share with all these other people I was meeting who weren't over their ex either? What did it really take to mend a broken heart? I knew there's not any one-size-fits-all-approach that could heal heartbreak; but was there a formula that would work for most people?

Obviously, I already had some answers. After all, I had been dishing out breakup advice since the days my friends and I began dating as teenagers in the North Jersey suburbs. Back then, I knew how to help a girl get over an ex by finding a new boy who would crush on her. (Hint: It involved the girl having a parent carpool her group of girlfriends to Teen Night at a local club, a for-the-car-ride-only-cardigan that'd be shed to display revealing "club clothes" as soon as the girls entered the club and the girl seductively shaking her booty to anything from Louie DeVito to Jay-Z.)

Been there, Done that

I eventually learned that I could make a thirty-something woman see that being dumped by that sorry excuse for a man was a blessing in disguise--despite the fact that her clock was ticking. I later realized that even the guy who swore to God that he'd never meet anyone as special as his ex could be convinced that he would, in fact, love again.

In my time spent helping friends and clients deal with the pain from their past relationships, I learned that there were many ways to approach the challenging task of getting over an ex. There were some things that worked better than others and some things that didn't do any good at all. I saw how challenging it was for some of my friends to say goodbye to their ex. I would watch them take two steps forward, followed by two steps backward. I would be as supportive as I could-which was seriously supportive-despite my frustration with their heart's tenacious grip on the "douche bag ex boyfriend," "psycho ex girlfriend," or simply "the one who got away". However, I never had as much empathy for the brokenhearted until I had to go through the horrors myself. It was only then that I could say I truly knew how it felt to think there was no getting over someone, to doubt that feelings for an ex would ever go away, and to consider the possibility of ending up alone with cats a real one. It was only then that my idea of writing this book to help people rise above their breakups was born.

I wanted to come up with some solid solutions to inspire the men and women that were really struggling to get over past relationships and deliver them in a fun and entertaining fashion. I wanted to hold their hands every step of the way. I wanted to make them laugh. Make them cry. Make them know there is someone out there who gets it. To say the things that would make them feel better--the things that their mom, dad, sisters, brothers, and best friends didn't know how to say. To make them see that every ending is a new beginning. Help them understand that their breakup is a chance to go all or nothing. To fight or flight. To ride or die. To go big or go home. I wanted to encourage them to dig deeper and to learn their lessons well so they'd never again date someone who was their ex in different packaging. I wanted to help them find out what they were really made of. To inspire them to ask for help. To hold on. To give up. To have hope. To lose hope. To let go of the past. To live in the present. To create a brighter future. And most importantly, to open their hearts again.

The Rx for Heartbreak-- Italian American Style

Instinctively, I knew just how to pull off all that jazz. My strategy would be Italian American style, of course. Being seventy-five percent Italian and growing up in a town where just about everyone had macaroni and meatballs for Sunday dinner, I was immersed in the culture. As a child, I thought everyone was Italian. In fact, it even seemed that my Hungarian grandfather acted pretty Italian American too. Didn't all families have a basement kitchen with six bottles of olive oil in the pantry? Weren't "talking" and "yelling" synonymous for all Italian American parents? *Who knew there were volumes besides loud and louder?* Didn't all kids have an Uncle Joey?

As a teenager, I learned that being Italian American meant more than just making your confirmation, going to the Jersey Shore, and hooking up with a guy named Vinnie. (For the record, I did all of the above, but I was no Snooki!) Growing up, Italian American meant learning the definition of respect, having family loyalty, and realizing that food is love. It meant feeling bad if you did not give goodbye kisses to all who attended family parties, having super strict parents, and only dating those whose last name ended in a vowel. As a young adult, it meant laughing at both the truth and the stereotypes in the shows that poked fun at Italian American culture including my favorites *The Sopranos, Jersey Shore, Mob Wives*, and *The Real Housewives of NJ*. As an Italian American woman, I came to some very important realizations—namely that everything really is better with cheese and that I probably would marry an Italian despite my beloved Grandma Lu Lu's repetitive suggestion not to. *Keyword: Probably.*

Italian American is what I know, and it is only natural that I'd want to share my culture in a way that could benefit others. I realized there are aspects of Italian American culture that helped me mend my broken heart, and I was determined to make my methods be known.

Just as I began writing How *to Get Over Your Ex: A Step By Step Guide to Mend a Broken Heart—Italian American Style*, I realized there was one small problem. *Shit.* I wasn't really over my ex enough to be writing a how-to-get-over-an-ex-book. I mean, I thought was. On the surface, I had clearly moved on. I did all the "right" things that one attempting to get over an ex was supposed to do:

- I deleted Facebook photos and emails

- I was focusing on my career

- I was dating (a lot of) new guys

- Keeping fit with yoga, Zumba, and nights out on the town

- Socializing with good friends

.... and generally enjoying life.

I thought I had gotten "closure" about a half dozen times. Yet on a few occasions, my head and heart would still debate. *Maybe closure is a myth?* While I intellectually understood it was best to cut the cord, my heart was still hanging on. Going back would feel like relapsing--like I was giving into some urge, almost as if I was a drug addict craving another hit. People do say that love is like heroine. (This sounds dramatic, but if you've ever been on and off with someone, you know how addictive the dynamic can be!)

At other times, it wasn't so serious--at least nothing a fun night out in a hot little black dress couldn't fix. But when the music stopped, the party ended, and I'd lie awake in my bed, I looked deep down into my heart. It was obvious I still had some healing to do.

Sure, people teach what they need to learn. I knew I'd rather teach other people how to get over their exes than sound like a broken record talking about my own heartbreak. But it was too soon to be writing a book about an issue that I was still struggling with. I wasn't very far into the writing process when I realized that I really didn't feel comfortable telling people to cut all contact with their ex when I was still tempted to Facebook and Twitter stalk mine. *Okay, okay. There was a time I, too, did some stalking. Come on now, I am a Dating & Relationship Maven--not God!*

Clearly, I had a horrible case of writer's block. Not only would I let social invitations distract me from finishing this book, but I would find household chores to do that didn't even need to be done. I knew I had a problem when I'd rather clean a toilet than finish a chapter. It was then I realized I was at a stalemate—just like I had been in my failed relationships. When I took an honest look into my psyche, I had an epiphany. It was almost as if all I wanted was to write this book as a declaration of independence from all of my exes; as if I was saying: "Ha! I'm over you. And I wrote a book to prove it." That's when I knew that I had no business writing this book at that time. I was an Italian American who wanted to get in the last word, but it was time to stai zitto. (Shut up.)

The journey of trying to get over an ex has taught me you can't just put pressure on yourself to do a little work and think you'll be over a relationship on your desired timeline. Ending love-like falling in love-isn't really a linear process. (Notice it is called *falling* in love and not *planning* to fall in love!) Now don't get me wrong, you will need to work hard and take logical steps in order to successfully move forward, but you can't be unrealistic and think you'll be cured when you want to be. Patience, my child.

Baby Steps in Your Quest to Get Over Your Ex

Full Disclosure: *How to Get Over Your Ex: A Step By Step Guide to Mend a Broken Heart--Italian American Style* does not provide an overnight, miracle cure. Anyone who tells you that you can get over a relationship faster than a New York minute is a liar or has never been in love. I believe in the cliché that anything in life worth doing takes some time to do, and healing your heart is no exception. Yes, I have felt the need for a quick fix just as much as the next girl who lost at the love game; but when you go out desperately searching for a quick fix, you usually end up with a hangover the size of Rome. However, when you go out without expectations, to say, casually meet a friend for a glass of vino to ease the pain, you usually find yourself a fabulous evening, complete with free drinks--which always taste better!

In all seriousness, don't underestimate what a long, hard process getting over an ex can be. For many, breakups are like experiencing a death of a loved one and can hurt more than any physical or emotional pain they've ever experienced. Just as in dealing with a death, when recovering from a breakup, people need to let themselves go through the stages of denial, anger, bargaining, and sadness before they can come to acceptance. That doesn't sound like a process one could easily expedite, huh? And why should it be? After all, Rome wasn't built in a day.

The people who try to just put a band aid on a broken heart end up getting hurt more deeply in the long run. If you ditch your desire for a quick fix and just take baby steps in your quest to mend up all that wear and tear, you won't do any additional damage. The actual repair of your broken heart will be the result of all the mending action this book will teach you to take. There will literally be action steps for you to take at the end of each chapter, so read each chapter in the order that it was written and complete the assignments. By reading this book, you have shown that you are ready to put on your big boy or big girl panties and make the kind of commitment to yourself that your ex could never make to you. This is a commitment to your recovery. Yes, *recovery.*

As one my exes said: “Having an unhealthy relationship is like having cancer. Breaking up is like removing the tumor.” Your relationship wouldn’t have ended if it was totally healthy-- just like you wouldn’t have a cancerous tumor if you were in perfect health. I know you couldn’t live with that tumor-or your ex-for much longer, but I promise that you can definitely live a long time without them!

After a surgery, a patient needs to recover, and so do you. The stress of a breakup and the lack of sleep and tears that typically come with it, wreak havoc on your immune system. The good news is: It doesn’t hurt indefinitely; you WILL get through this and be healthy again! It is just super important that you start taking care of your physical and mental health so you can get well soon.

Kelly Clarkson got it right. Whatever doesn’t kill you really does make you stronger. (And she isn’t even Italian American!) So, grab your box of tissues, pour yourself some Pinot Grigio, and let this Italian American bella teach you how to come back swinging.

P.S. Is it just me or does it already feel like we are paisanos?

Step 1:

Forgetaboutit: Realize Your Relationship Just Got Whacked

Your mission, should you choose to accept it, starts with mourning the death of your relationship.

Take a deep breath.

Your relationship is over.

Breathe in.

It has all come to an end.

Breathe out.

No, really, things with your ex are dead and will never be the same.

Breathe again. Deeper.

I know that this is hard to hear, but it is my job to give you some tough love. My goal is to tell it like it is and give you the goods upfront, so I can shorten your pain like they shortened an Italian last name on Ellis Island!

Okay, chances are, your life is not like an episode of *The Sopranos*, and there was no mob boss who decided your ex had to get whacked.

Whether you decided to let go of him or her, got dumped, or were in a relationship in which the decision was mutual, you found yourself at the end of the road. No matter how things go down, breakups are rough. Love kills. Relationships die. Hearts get broken.

Repeat after me, right this second: I AM NOT BROKEN.

Doesn't sound very convincing yet, huh?

Can I get another: I AM NOT BROKEN?

Your relationship is broken though, and the aftermath is going to hurt.

Accepting things are over is no easy task. If you did not see any warning signs that your relationship was going downhill, it is likely that you are in denial that your relationship is truly broken. Being blindsided is common--especially for men. (This definitely applies to married men, as research shows it is women who typically file for divorce.) You may minimize how unhealthy your dynamic was, or make excuses for your ex's bad behavior. You may think the relationship can be fixed-especially if you were together a long time-or that you are going through a "break" and not a breakup. Even if you saw red flags, it can be hard to admit that things have really come to an end. Your ex's decision to split could have come as a shock to you or you just might not be able to wrap your head around never being able to go on dates or sleep with your ex again. If you were talking about spending your life together, it can be even harder to accept that the two of you are walking away instead of down the aisle.

It is difficult just to process what has happened in the days after a breakup. Your brain is foggy, and your heart is heavy. *Ugggh.* I totally get it. You are hurting, and I am truly sorry for your loss. You are soon going to have to try to forget about your relationship. You are probably thinking "How could I forget about it when everything reminds me of my ex?" Now that we are on the subject, it is totally normal to be relating everything to your ex right now. The teller at the bank that looked like your ex. The iced cappuccino that you last had with your ex. The Giorgio Armani cologne or Gucci perfume that smelled just like your ex. You will be thinking about your ex as you read this book, and you may be thinking about your ex when you finish reading this book.

Trust me; I know how hard it is. Chances are you may come to believe that there is nothing in the world as excruciatingly painful as losing someone you love--that is, until you realize you would rather projectile vomit than picture that person with someone else. *Yes, I've been there too.* Let me give it to you straight like any true Italian American would: You are going to feel like crap. For a while. It's just the way the story goes. The reality of your situation is that life as you knew it has come to an end. I cannot stress this enough: A breakup is like a death.

The Grief Phase--Italian American Style

When a relationship dies, you *should* feel like you are mourning a loss. Not only did you lose your ex-and perhaps a part of yourself-but you also lost the ability to go to all those places you used to love going to with your ex. That restaurant where you had your first date? The club where you first kissed? The part of Florida where you had your first vacation? *Yup, ruined forever. Or umm, at least dead to you for now.*

Speaking of death, you'll probably look and feel like it immediately after a breakup when you are going to go through different stages of the mourning process, starting with denial. Eventually, you are going to start feeling better. And then you are going to feel like crap again. If you choose to see your ex before it is safe to do so, you are going to get even more caught up in this vicious cycle. *Rinse & Repeat, much?* Too much breakup and makeup with your ex, and it won't be long until you start airing your dirty laundry like those Italian American neighbors who literally put it all up on a clothesline for everyone to see. It is tempting to talk about your drama with anyone and everyone who will listen. *And when they are sick of hearing it, you just find new people who aren't.* But there comes a point in which you must ask yourself: Do I really need an entire village to know my business?

In the aftermath of a breakup, there is a lot you need to forget about. (The less people you tell, the less people to remind you of it all.)You shouldn't even be communicating with your ex at all. (Much more on that later.) You should just be mourning. Your ex is not dead, but he or she might as well be dead to you---at least for a good chunk of time and possibly forever.

Grieving is completely acceptable if you are getting over your ex Italian American style. As a rule of thumb, we Italian Americans are very passionate people. We are loud, emotional, and probably just talking at a normal volume when our friends of other ethnic groups think we are screaming. A death in an Italian American family--and the traditions that follow--is typically a pretty big deal. Not only is there a lot of planning that goes into the wake, funeral, and repast, there is a likelihood that the death will really change things in a profound way. (Think holidays never being the same, and, ah, yes, family dynamics changing due to fights about wills and dividing the Estate.)

For Italian Americans experiencing a death of a loved one, mourning is the norm. It is a time we wear black, cry, and have people send fruit baskets to our home. Grieving is hard and embracing the mourning process helps us cope with the loss.

Don't think this isn't a process. When you go through a breakup--just like when you are dealing with the death of a loved one--you can't decide to grieve for a day and be done with it. You can't just turn your feelings on and off like a faucet. You might be able to turn off the sadness or lower its volume when you need to function at work or with friends, but it is likely your despair will come back again. After all, your relationship may be dead, but the memories and feelings live on—though the intensity of the awful feelings will weaken in time. It is best to realize that these emotions will fade in and out of your life for a while. Feelings for your ex may not completely go away, but you need to accept that the relationship is over and you have to move on despite them. You can love your ex all you want from a distance, but it does not mean that you should or will be together.

I know that once you come to a place of acceptance about your failed relationship you can survive and thrive after your breakup, because I have seen countless men and women do it. I've helped many of them move on before I even helped myself move on. For the record, it wasn't *too* long before I helped myself move on, but it took a lot more time than I anticipated. Being a dating and relationship expert doesn't make a girl immune to wounds in the battlefield of love. Unfortunately, it wasn't a piece of (Italian cream) cake for me, and it won't be for you.

No matter who you are, getting over an ex you really loved just isn't as easy as Badda Bing, Badda Boom. It is easier though if you take the right actions. Moving forward means taking immediate and proper action that is in line with the current reality that your relationship must be left in the past. Therefore, the very first thing you should do is understand that your relationship got whacked and that you need to manage your expectations about the process of getting over your ex. Treating a breakup like a death is one of the best things you can do for yourself, but only if you really embrace this notion.

First, acknowledge that the breakup should be permanent--even if you love your ex. You may know a couple who had a horrible breakup and got back together and seem to be doing just fine. I hate to burst your bubble, but they are an exception and not the rule. Love is messy, and a lot of messes just can't be cleaned up. Pain can come with any stage of love, but the ending love part is what can really do you and your relationship dirty. *Not as dirty as the mob; but let's just say nobody gets out unscathed.* Relationships are diverse, but when they break, the people in them can get pretty crazy.

One of the craziest things people do--besides calling an ex ten times in a row--is try and fix unhealthy relationships that can never really be fixed. The kinds of unhealthy relationships people try to save range from dull and unfulfilling, to ones that are broken beyond repair. I am talking about the type of relationships that have your friends and family members shaking their heads in disbelief. The relationships that inspire random strangers who catch you crying in public bathrooms to say sympathetic things like "It shouldn't be so hard."

When it becomes obvious that your relationship has gone bad, there is really only one good option: Forgetaboutit! You wouldn't drink milk that went bad in hope it'd change its form, now would you? When relationships turn sour and love starts to hurt, you have to realize that things most likely aren't going to work out. Most exes do not come back to each other and live happily ever after. Even if your ex comes back, it does not mean you will be happy together.

And, by the way, the plot of *The Notebook* is totally ridiculous! (Sorry Ryan Gosling; I would still birth your children!) If you just had a breakup, stay away from this movie. Now is just not the time for you to watch a movie about a guy creepy enough to wait around for an ex and build a house for her while she is getting ready to marry someone else. This stuff doesn't happen in real life. Okay, so technically some of your exes may come back. (Mine sure as hell did. *All of them. Sigh.*) But even if your ex does come back, you need to think your ex is not coming back.

In the meantime, keep reading, because I have some advice on the inevitable run in with an ex later…

So, basically, unless you believe in reincarnation, chances are your ex is not coming back to be with you forever. You can think that you were connected in past lives all you want, but you aren't going to let such impact your present reality, because you are supposed to be making like an Italian American. Kindly note: Anyone whose ancestors came from the boot shaped country weren't taught to believe in "that crap". The fact is that in the present, your relationship has run its course. So……...

Forgetaboutit!

There are many things in life that end or change. Consequently, you are going to have to give up some of your old behaviors that reflect this new way of thinking about your relationship. While everyone is different, there are many things that most people need to forget about when healing a broken heart.

What you need to give up most are those behaviors that keep you stuck on your ex and give you false hope your relationship will work, as well as those that make you feel bad and hopeless about your future. There are common things that people do post breakup that lead to self-sabotage. You may be tempted to do some of these things, but you must avoid them at all costs. I will go into more detail about these things shortly, but for now, just recognize that they are counterproductive, and you will have to eliminate them from your life.

Wondering what you must forget about?

Without further ado, here are "My Fifty Shades of Forgetaboutit!"

You should not be:

1. Reminiscing over special times (There are better things you could have done than spend so much time with your ex, right? Likewise, your time would now be best spent creating an amazing life.)

2. Thinking you will never meet someone as special as your ex again (Sorry, your ex isn't that special.)

3. Thinking "out of sight out of mind" is a myth (Distance does help, eventually.)

4. Seeing your relationship as a waste of time (There are lessons you learned.)

5. Having unrealistic expectations about how fast you'll heal. (It is going to take some time.)

6. Feeling so alone (You aren't the first person to suffer from heartbreak, and you won't be the last. Think about it: All relationships eventually end.)

7. Thinking you won't get teary over little things (You will become more emotional post-breakup.)

8. Listening to songs that depress you and remind you of your ex (Create a new uplifting playlist.).

9. Going to psychics to see what they can tell you about your ex (This can become a vicious cycle. If you are so attached to the idea of your ex, you will just keep going to different psychics until one tells you something that you like!)

10. Wanting someone who doesn't want you

11. Wanting someone who has moved on with someone else

12. Believing one more conversation will give you all the closure you need (More likely, it will just open an old or all new can of tomato sauce.)

13. Fantasizing about the perfect breakup (Relationships don't begin and end the way you want them to.)

14. Basing your moods on how your ex treats you (Your ex might treat you like shit, but it is up to you to decide whether or not you will allow yourself to feel like shit.)

15. Hoping for the happy ending (Helllllo, this isn't *The Notebook.)*

16. Needing to prove you were right in the relationship or about the relationship

17. Blaming everyone and anyone else for the end of your relationship

18. Believing you can fix your ex (You can't fix anyone. *Period.*)

19. Thinking you won't be able to live without your ex (Life will go on.)

20. Wearing out your welcome with friends (It happens. There will come a point where they get sick of hearing you talk about your ex.)

21. Remaining good friends with your ex's friends (If your ex isn't in your life anymore, why should his friends be getting your attention?)

22. Thinking you can decide the last time you will cry over your ex

23. Analyzing all the reasons why your ex has moved on without you

24. Comparing your ex to new men/women you meet and thinking your ex is better

25. Letting your doubt that you will find a new relationship lead you right back to your ex

26. Putting the relationship up on a pedestal (Don't see your relationship through rose-colored glasses.)

27. Staring at your phone and hating it when there are no new messages (Stop getting disappointed every time the phone rings, and it is not your ex. This is toxic!)

28. Drunk-dialing your ex

29. Calling your ex while sober (The emotional hangover is even more terrible.)

30. Emailing your ex

31. Texting your ex

32. Stalking your ex's Facebook, Twitter, LinkedIn, Myspace, FourSquared, and Instagram accounts

33. Stalking your ex's friends on said social networking sites

34. Having rebound sex

35. Finding excuses not to shower, exercise, or otherwise take care of yourself.

36. Avoiding all your friends

37. Going back again for another pink slip (Do you really want to give your ex the opportunity to reject you again?)

38. Wondering if your ex has changed

39. Wondering if your ex loves someone else more than he/she loved you.
40. Wondering if you were the best sex your ex ever had
41. Thinking your ex is the best sex you've ever had
42. Keeping photos of your ex in your home (You do not need to be reminded of your ex multiple times every day.)
43. Failing to erase all the photos albums of you and your ex on Facebook
44. Calling your ex's mother or sister "just to say hi"
45. Bringing up your ex in conversation every time someone starts talking about dating or relationships
46. Calling your ex from blocked numbers just to hear his or her voicemail
47. Checking your ex's old accounts (Amazon, phone bill, email, etc.) that you may still have passwords for
48. Having joint custody of an animal with your ex (Someone just needs to take the pet.)
49. Trying to live together until the home you co-own cells
50. Beating yourself up because you are frustrated every time you have a setback

Action Steps To Help You Realize Your Relationship Just Got Whacked

Get rid of the evidence.

You don't have to be Mafioso to know you've got to do *away* with anything that would prove you are guilty of a crime. You know what should be a crime? Holding on to photos and objects that remind you of your ex. The last thing you need is to be reminded of your ex with a look at your phone, computer, or around your home. You do not need to see the images of the two of you in happier times. Seeing them will only activate the part of your brain that makes you long for your ex. If you can't bear to box up the photos, at least put them in a drawer that you don't open. If you are really brave, you can do what some people swear by--*burn them.*

You may not want to delete photos from your social media pages, but you should strongly consider doing the inevitable sooner rather than later. Just save the images on a CD or flash drive so you can look at them at a much later time. The random objects, gifts, or pieces of clothing that remind you of your ex or belong to your ex need to be dealt with. The best thing to do is just get them out of your sight. If you don't get rid of them, you are only holding on to pain.

Stai Zitto: Enforce a strict no contact policy.

That's right: Shut up, already! Cutting off all contact with your ex can be one of the most difficult parts of your recovery. Take it from the girl who has blocked and unblocked the same phone number way too many times, it is absolutely necessary for at least for the time being.

Contrary to all the breakup stories in *People* magazine, you should not try to be friends with your ex right away. It is naive and emotionally taxing to pretend you can instantly switch from romantic to platonic. Any premature attempt at friendship will cause more damage to your relationship, ego, heart, and maybe even your reputation. Speaking of damage, this is what will result if you text or email your ex at this time. If you do not adhere to this rule, you will discover that in retrospect, your words-whether they were written drunk or sober- will make you cringe. You are still extremely emotional and not thinking clearly about your ex. If you drunk-dial, your emotions are even more intense and your judgment even more impaired. This could lead to bad things such as having sex with an ex, which is clearly a MAJOR violation of the no contact rule.

Face it: There is really no reason to be in touch when the relationship is over and you are trying to get over it. You don't need to be there for your ex's needs; you need to tend to your own. If you are tempted to initiate contact--or have an ex who will--you need to call your phone company and block your ex's number. Then you need to block your ex--and possibly his or her friends and family--on Facebook, Twitter, email, etc. No contact means **no contact.**

Get real through the written word.

At this point, you need people and evidence to remind you of reality. It may be helpful to go back and read an email or text conversation leading up to the breakup. If you keep a journal, this is a perfect time to read old entries to get a clear picture of the demise of your relationship.

As someone who has kept journals since age 11, *I can't stress enough just how effective journaling post-breakup can be*. If you don't keep a journal, you should start writing in one, as it will help you keep track of your feelings and any interaction with your ex. It will be a tool to let go of the past and stay focused on the present reality. After all, if you wrote something down in black and white, you can't really deny that it was true.

Step 2:

Flip Tables & Cry: Get Mad & Sad--Because You Are Too Good For This

Once you realize your relationship is over, it is time to get in touch with your emotions. You need to become intimately acquainted with all of them--from anger to sadness--to move forward. Don't deny yourself the opportunity to feel your feelings. The sooner you realize that plenty of people want to burst into tears every time they hear a song that reminds them of their ex, the sooner you let yourself cry. Healing is all about understanding that your feelings are normal. Believe me, you are not a freak of nature for feeling like the world has come to an end. You are not a skank for not wanting to shower for three days. (But try to take one anyway.) You are not bipolar because you are going through the gamut of emotions.

A breakup can be a roller coaster ride in which you feel different every day. Your emotions are a slave to your life circumstances when you are recovering from a breakup. One minute you think you are fine, the next minute you are pulling over on the side of the highway bawling your eyes out. Oh and the minute after that, you are longing for your ex to comfort you, because you've never felt so hopeless. *No, you are not batshit crazy*. When you are mourning a tremendous loss, you are on a long road with a lot of twists and turns. You may think there is no rhyme or reason to the mourning process. You may even consider your emotions to be like visitors, as they tend to be inconsistent, coming and going as they please. Emotional instability is to be expected.

All of this emotional stuff can feel uncomfortable--especially for the boys. A breakup can make you feel mad or sad for longer than you'd prefer. Even stubborn Italian Americans who typically refuse to show weakness can be susceptible to depression at this time. Rest assured: "This too shall pass." But only if you get comfortable getting in touch with your emotions first.

Who better to teach you how to get emotional than the Italian Americans?

Here's a little not-so-secret-secret: Being such passionate people, we Italian Americans are known to display both tempers and tears. Regarding the tempers, it's not just *Real Housewives of NJ's* Teresa Giudice, who'd be flipping tables on national TV. Many Italian Americans are known to be hot heads that get loud, curse, and quickly anger when others disagree with their opinions. Italian American men punching holes in walls or sparring with their brothers, friends, and sometimes even their fathers is not a rare occurrence. These men- especially those who have very "old school" parents- are not the easiest to deal with. It isn't just the men who get angry. Yelling, screaming, and sudden displays of anger happen to women in this culture as well, but so does making up and crying happy tears soon after.

It is important to clarify that while Italian Americans get mad, it doesn't necessarily mean they get violent; though they are often portrayed as such due to their mob ties and presence in gangster movies. Despite what *Mob Wives* may lead you to believe, Italian Americans are not, at large, violent people who are caught up in "the lifestyle".

Most importantly, I am not suggesting anyone reading this book commits an act of violence. Not only is it morally wrong and absolutely disgusting to abuse people, animals, or oneself, it is stupid. Sure, you might be so mad at your ex that you think it'd feel great to take a swing, but what would that solve? Seriously, what did anyone ever get out of putting his or her dukes up besides a restraining order? *Do you really want to be reminded of you ex every time you fill out a job application?*

If you want to let your anger out on something, an inanimate object-like a punching bag- is the way to go. Be warned: I don't suggest actually flipping tables at home or in public places, but it is better than hurting an actual organism. While throwing furniture or kicking a hole in a wall may temporarily ease the rage, exercise is better. Some type of physical exercise like cardio, weight-lifting, or ideally kickboxing can give you a greater long term release. If you find that going to a shooting range or hitting golf balls while picturing your ex's face works for you, by all means, keep at it! Other healthy ways to express feelings of anger include venting to a friend on the phone, in person, or via email. Writing a "letter never sent" to your ex is also an also an ideal way to get your negative feelings out.

You should not be afraid to feel anger, because it is healthier in the long run to let out negative emotions than to keep them bottled up inside. Some cultures teach people to suppress anger, but I think they've got it all wrong. People who get angry realize their truth; they let it out and are free to be who they want to be. After the anger comes healing. Hence, I'm suggesting that you deal with your negative emotions in the way an Italian American would: Recognize you are angry and let it rip--in a healthy way that won't cause harm! If you don't acknowledge your anger, you stay stuck in that very first stage of the mourning process, denial. Although all the evidence that your relationship just got whacked is there, you will still hold on to the glimmers of hope when you are in denial. You will stay stuck in an unhealthy place.

Finding truth is something very important to Italian Americans, as they typically have big egos and don't like to be played. Truth is essential for self-development, and sometimes you have to get angry to grow spiritually. If you don't live authentically, you run the risk of becoming depressed. (After all, depression is just anger turned inward.) You also run the risk of the inevitable explosion on family and friends. (Just watch Season 5 of *Real Housewives of New Jersey* for plenty of evidence of Italian Americans doing this.) Don't take your pain out on those around you, because it can do a lot of harm. All of this destructive behavior can lead to cut off relationships at worst, and individual, couples, or family therapy at best. You don't have to go to psychotherapy to learn that it is beneficial for you to get in touch with your truth. You heard it here. Believe it! You should get in touch with your truth, and the truth is, if you have an ex, you probably have something to be angry about.

Anger certainly has its place when a relationship ends, so understand that you are normal for experiencing it since your relationship ended. Feelings of anger, which mark the second stage of the mourning process, will make you aware that you harbor rage toward your ex. You might become furious that he or she did not properly communicate their feelings, forgive you for your mistakes, or commit to you in the way you wanted. You might feel that you have been mistreated and can become enraged at the thought of your ex dating someone else. If you don't feel anger yet, you are probably still stuck in sadness and despair. In that case, you need something that will take away the longing for your ex and should consider adopting a bit of an Italian American temper.

Before you can get mad, you have to find something to be mad about. If you look to Italian American culture for clues, it isn't too hard to find something to be mad about, because Italian Americans can react to the littlest things. Some may think they are overdramatic, but others think their reactions are completely appropriate.

Consider a scene in one of the typical Italian American's all time favorite movies, Chazz Palminteri's, *A Bronx Tale*:

"Alright, listen to me. You pull up right where she lives, right? Before you get outta the car, you lock both doors. Then, get outta the car, you walk over to her. You bring her over to the car. Dig out the key, put it in the lock and open the door for her. Then you let her get in. Then you close the door. Then you walk around the back of the car and look through the rear window. If she doesn't reach over and lift up that button so that you can get in: dump her."

"Just like that?"

"Listen to me, kid. If she doesn't reach over and lift up that button so that you can get in, that means she's a selfish broad and all you're seeing is the tip of the iceberg. You dump her and you dump her fast."

Now, outside of the Italian American context it may seem silly to dump a girl because she didn't open the car door, but it actually makes total sense when you consider how proud Italian Americans are. We want to be respected, because we have a lot to be respected for. (Keep reading for evidence of all our accomplishments!)

Naturally, an Italian American guy deserves a girl who cares enough to make his life easier with a gesture as simple as opening a door. In a typical Italian American guy's eyes, anyone who doesn't see his greatness should not be tolerated. (If they aren't for him, they are against him.) Do you see the reason why those in a culture where there is this much pride would get mad at someone like your ex?

Chances are, a true Italian American would even call your ex a *stunad.*

It would help if you, too, come to believe that your ex is "a stunad" or someone more commonly known as stupid. So what if he or she went to Harvard! Anyone who doesn't recognize what a prize you are is displaying considerable evidence of stupidity. Failing to appreciate you or not recognizing what you both had until it was gone is just plain STUPID.

Seriously, you are fabulous—and not just because you are (wo)man enough to read a self-help book when you need it. We are all unique individuals with a story to tell. We all have value, and we are all worthy of love. Even your ex. However, right now, I want you to think of your ex as nothing more than a stunad. It is incredibly helpful to regard him or her as stupid, because then you'll stop blaming yourself so much. Don't get me wrong, two people play a role in the success or failure of a relationship. It is important to realize the mistakes that you made and learn from them so that you don't make the same ones in your next relationship. There is a time and place for that. It is not now.

We will get to you considering the part you played in the death of your relationship shortly, but for now, just stay focused on your ex's stupidity. With this in mind, you can stop replaying all the last conversations in your head. *Over and over again.* Your effort to figure out what went wrong is respectable, but let it go. If you find yourself hung up on finding the reasons, know that this is normal. It makes sense that you'd want this closure, but it is unlikely that you are ever going to fully get the closure you need from a conversation with your ex—or worse, from a conversation with yourself in your head. Something that may make you feel better is the recognition of a universal truth among dating & relationship coaches like yours truly: It's hardly ever just one thing you did that ruined the spaghetti sauce, and it is likely a combination of reasons why your relationship failed. It can seem like there is one thing you or your stupid ex did that ruined it all. Having an affair with your ex's best friend, for example, could easily lead to your scarlet letter, but a lot of times it is more complicated than that. (After all, a lot of couples stay together through all sorts of horrible things, and infidelity is no exception.) Just keep in mind, nothing could have gone *so* wrong as to destroy a relationship that was truly meant to be.

If your ex wasn't so stupid, maybe your relationship would have worked. Maybe your ex should have worn one of those Italian horn necklaces for protection against the evil eye or said the rosary a few more times.

But your ex didn't, and now it's over. Do you really want to go back to a stunad? Think about it! What kind of impact would being in a relationship with someone who is not a smart person have on your life? Could it cause financial or legal problems, mental stress and disease, alienation from friends and family? Grief? Premature aging? I don't know about you, but the last type of relationship I want to be in is one that gives me headaches, dark under eye circles, and wrinkles! In fact, I want to be a hot mama before and after I potentially pop out a new generation of Antonius and Alessandria's. *I want to raise children, not men.....*

Dating or getting married to someone stunad is most likely going to be a continuous cycle of heartbreak, because stunads are usually very selfish. It is no fun to be in a relationship with someone who is selfish, because that person will rarely take your needs into consideration. It will be as if your needs don't even exist. After all, your stunad ex broke your heart once, what makes you think he or she wouldn't break it again?

There is a common denominator among stunad exes. They are selfish, immature, and see the world only through their eyes. They'll think more about what they want than what is good for you and the relationship as a whole. They are usually poor communicators who never really understand their emotional needs—let alone your emotional needs. With a stunad, you never really feel understood or taken care of. You may feel like you have to fight to get what you want out of the partnership, and at times, you won't feel like you have a partnership at all. Stunad exes keep you guessing and never allow you to feel secure with where your relationship stands. They purposely wait hours to answer your text messages, don't call you back until a day or two later, fail to make plans, cancel the plans they rarely make, and act like hotheads. They are the types that take a long time to make a relationship "official," leave their brides or grooms at the altar, and never realize how much they loved you until they lost you. *Oh, and they are selfish in bed.*

Not very appealing, huh? If you met your ex now and knew his or her true stunad colors, you would run pretty fast, right? Whatever your mode of transportation, just get the hell out of there! Pull a Beyoncé and realize the good in goodbye! (Again, another non-Italian American singer with some inspirational lyrics.)

You might want to stop and think about why you ended up with such a stunad ex in the first place. It is probably a simple reason--like you have a big heart and the patience of a saint! Or maybe your opposite sex parent is a stunad, so it felt familiar and therefore desirable to you. Or maybe your stunad got "grandfathered" in by spending considerable time with you in your precious young years. *Oops, was that just me? Oh, young love!* Regardless of how your love relationship began, love is hard to end—especially when it is for the first time. If you want to get over your ex and move on to the next, realize a stunad does not change his stripes.

Face the facts: You fell in love with someone stupid, and naturally, the relationship's shelf life was short. Even if you don't believe your ex is a stunad, you've got to believe he or she is now a stupid choice for you. If you start to think you could fix your stunad ex, just stop right there; because then you will become the real stunad! You can't fix stupid, so don't bother trying!

The Action Steps at the end of this chapter will help you avoid turning into a stunad yourself. Open your eyes to your ex's true colors, and you should be able to scream, shout, and let it all out!

After you get the anger out, you'll want to *calm down.* You can have some herbal tea, or do it the Italian American way and find yourself a nice vintage bottle of vino. You can light candles and meditate. Listen to positive, uplifting music or even take a warm, bubble bath or shower. When things slow down and you start feeling calm, don't be surprised if you start thinking about your ex in a different way. After the anger subsides, you'll transition into the bargaining phase of the grieving process. It will feel pretty similar to how you were when you were in denial, but you will take it a step further. You will wrack your brain for every possible way to make your failed relationship work.

For instance, you'll think that maybe your parents, best friend, priest, rabbi, etc. can talk some sense into your ex. Maybe you'll even start bargaining with God. *You know if he just brings your ex back for a quick reunion you'll donate a fourth of your salary to charity every month.* Without a doubt, at this point, you are getting very desperate.

Pretty sad, huh? Are you crying yet?

I give you permission to cry, because that is what is natural when a loss occurs. Crying enables you to step out of the denial and bargaining stage and into the reality of what just happened.

You might shed a few tears or you might want to curl up into the fetal position and cry for days. You might sleep until your back hurts from sleeping so much and only stop when you realize you don't want to sleep your life away. But before you come to that conclusion, you will either lose your appetite or eat all the Eggplant Parmesan sandwiches and slices of Sicilian your local pizza joint has to offer. You will then need to go to the supermarket to buy chamomile tea bags or cucumbers to soothe your puffy, bloodshot eyes. If you are like I once was, you may even text a photo of your conjunctivitis to your ex. He or she will say something stupid that won't make you feel better. Something like "Eyes can't be beautiful if they haven't cried." *Okay, none of your exes nor mine would ever say anything like that, but it is true.* In fact, this sentiment is so true that these days I'd barely consider dating a man who hasn't had his heart broken at least once. There really is beauty in heartbreak, but it is not all that helpful of a realization when you are feeling about as beautiful as an eighty-five year old Nonna slaving over a hot stove and wiping the sweat off her brow. Got a mental picture of that? *Look, the comments from your ex would probably be pretty cliché, so I'm just trying not to be.*

For a considerable chunk of time, it is likely that there won't be a day that goes by without you thinking of him or her and getting sad, and that is okay. Sad feelings linger. Sometimes they go away and then creep back up on you. When you think of all the good times and the happiness you felt when you were in the relationship, you'll become sad about everything from the fact that it didn't work out to how it ended.

Just when you think you can't be any more depressed, you may start to feel either more depressed, angry, or even apathetic. In moments of quiet, you will hopefully start to believe that you didn't deserve to be treated the way your ex treated you. Despite all of your emotions, there *is* a light at the end of the tunnel. You will not see it until you see yourself all the way to the acceptance stage of the grieving process. For now, you've got to keep on emoting.

Action Steps To Get Mad, Sad, And Realize You Are Too Good For This

Go to a bookstore and walk out empowered.

A trip to the self-help section can really solidify two important lessons. 1. You are a great catch. 2. Your ex is a stunad. I know. I know. This may appeal more to the girls than the boys. Let's face it: Most modern day women have found themselves in the self-help section of Barnes & Noble with bloodshot eyes and a pack of tissues at least once in their life. (Guys, thank God for eBooks. Now, you can read and cry in the privacy of your own home!) Regardless of whether you are on the pink or blue team, if you've ever searched for the perfect book to mend your broken heart, you probably learned that breakup guides, like baked ziti, are not all created equal. Most breakup books are not as refreshingly honest yet entertaining and helpful as this one. You're welcome. I am just repping "my peeps". As I mentioned before, we Italian Americans are proud. *Maybe it is time I whip out my "Everybody Loves an Italian Girl" shirt from 2005?*

Anyway, even though some breakup books are just recycle the same tired advice, it wouldn't kill you to read a few more books on the subject. Any sassy lady or refined gent who wants to leave the past in the past and move forward with dignity, knows that knowledge is power. You need knowledge that will increase your self-esteem and give you confidence in your future. Look for books that help you realize how great you are. Know why you should be both mad and sad that you invested your time, energy, and heart into your stunad ex.

Make a list of all the reasons why your ex is a stunad.

A helpful activity is to make a list of all the reasons why your ex is a stunad. If you were dumped or forced to dump the person you love(d) because he or she was so stunad, you can review this list to understand exactly why your relationship was doomed. If you have trouble coming up with this list, you may have been in deep denial throughout your relationship and are probably still blinded by love.

If you are having difficulty pinpointing the exact reasons why your ex was such a stunad, just ask your friends and family. If you opened up to them in the slightest about your relationship problems or even if they have just seen your pain, I am sure they will have an earful for you!

Evaluate your ex by considering some common stunad red flags.

Call it a perk of the job, but my work has given me plenty of insight as to why exes are stupid. From a psychological perspective, I know sharing these reasons will make you feel better, as you will feel less alone. There is strength in numbers, for sure.

Knowing that other people have stunad exes and that their exes are stupid for the same reasons as your ex will be quite comforting, because it validates that you are a normal person.

Besides, the lists that follow will help you jog your memory, as there will probably be some parallels between the way your ex treated you and the way other people were treated by their exes.

Here are some signs of a stunad male ex:

1. *He is not responding to you.* If you are calling, emailing, and texting a guy, and it becomes clear that responding to you is not a priority. Therefore, you should not even have to ask how invested in the relationship he is. If a man is truly interested, he will make that clear to you. He will look forward to any contact from you and find every opportunity to respond—no matter how busy he may be.

2. *He is not calling you.* Sure, there are many men who prefer the convenience of texting to calling a woman they are dating, and he may not be “a phone person”. However, if he were falling for you, he’d want

to hear your voice as much as possible and certainly couldn't go too long without speaking if he was in love.

3. *He doesn't want to hang out with you during the day.* If the guy you are "dating" only wants to see you when it is dark out, he is probably only interested in getting you in between the sheets. If he really cared about you like a man who really cares about a woman does, he would want to spend time getting to know you in a different context. Like in public, during daylight.

4. *He won't introduce you to his friends.* Nearly all men want their friends to approve of the girl that they are dating. If he doesn't care to introduce you to his friends after a couple months of seeing each other, he probably doesn't care about dating you for the long term.

5. *He can't commit to plans.* A guy who wants to be with you will ask you out in advance to ensure that he will have the chance to see you. If he can never plan ahead of time, you may just be his Plan B. If you are initiating plans and he is consistently turning them down, this may be one of the strongest ten signs to know that he is not interested.

6. *He says he is not looking for anything serious.* When a man tells you that he does not want a girlfriend, you should believe him. He is either not in the right frame of mind or time in his life or he is not looking for anything serious with you. Either way, don't ignore this sign and think you can change his mind.

7. *He puts minimal effort into dates.* If he is not trying to impress you, it has not occurred to him that you are worth impressing! If all he can do is make vague last minute plans that require spending little energy and money, consider this a major clue in figuring out where you stand in the relationship. If he thinks you should schlep to see him, tell him you don't schlep. Men will schlep to you, but only if they are interested.

8. *He doesn't acknowledge holidays.* If it is a major holiday and he is not wishing you a happy one let alone asking you to spend it with him, he is definitely not thinking of you as girlfriend material. Men know that

the holidays are important to women. If he isn't acknowledging them and buying you gifts, it is because he doesn't want the relationship to get any more serious.

9. *He isn't initiating sex.* All guys want to have sex with a woman they are attracted to—unless they are saving themselves for marriage, of course. If he is not trying to sleep with you, he sees you as a platonic friend or has lost interest in sex with you. Period.

10. *He is seeing other women.* If a guy lets you know that he talks to and dates other women, he is probably sleeping with them too. If he's so involved with other women, he can't be so interested in committing to you. If he was really into you, it wouldn't take long before he would be seeing only you.

Here are the signs of a stunad female:

1. *She's ridiculously jealous.* There is something to be said for a reasonable amount of jealousy in a relationship. A woman who truly cares is protective of her man and wants him all to herself. But then there is the kind of jealousy that results from never getting over the ex that makes women insecure or deeply mistrustful of others. All this leads to is cell phone-checking-paranoia every time you leave the room.

2. *She doesn't respect your time.* Everyone just needs some time to themselves every now and again. If she feels that your whole schedule should be focused on time with her, especially in the beginning of a relationship, she will rob you of your independence and desire for her. Remember that absence makes the heart grow fonder.

3. *She constantly acts like your mother.* Women know that men do typically look for someone that has their mother's good qualities. However, women that think men are looking for another mother got it twisted. Any girl who thinks men need to be told what to do-and when to do it-is just plain stunad.

4. *She's super boring.* The woman who is closed-minded and unwilling to just try it once for you won't make you happy in the long run. She's too stunad to realize that couples bond over new experiences. She will inevitably annoy you to the point that you can't tolerate her, simply because you'll feel smothered-or bored to tears-by a woman who doesn't have a life of her own.

5. *She's constantly fishing for compliments.* A woman who is not confident and comfortable in her own skin should realize that she needs to work on herself before she can be attractive to you. If she doesn't love herself, she will be unable to love you.

6. *She doesn't communicate her needs and blames relationship problems on you.* A woman who expects you to be a mind reader is a woman you don't need in your life. If she doesn't speak up, her unhappiness is her fault. You can't fix what you don't know is broken.

7. *She lies to you.* If she doesn't have the decency to tell you the truth, she is no good. Enough said.

8. *She is not supportive of your dreams.* If she puts you down instead of lifting you up, your relationship is destined for failure. Instead of constantly thinking about she wants, she should try thinking about what is best for your relationship as a whole.

9. *She is involved with other men.* If she does not make you feel like a priority, you should not waste your time competing for her attention. If she surrounds herself with guy friends and male admirers more often than not, does she really want a monogamous relationship with you?

10. *She's a downer.* If you do not enjoy your time with her, because she is always complaining about petty things and acting in negative ways, you'd be better off without her. Who needs the drama?

Do you recognize that your ex sports any of these undesirable characteristics? If so, you are well on your way towards mending your broken heart. If you adopt a philosophy of stubbornness, eventually it will become a part of your personality just like it is a part of Italian American culture. When you are still early on in the heart healing process-like when you are in the bargaining stage-there will be times when you are tempted to do things that you shouldn't in regard to your ex. You will think counterproductive things like "Maybe I really am capable of being her friend" or "I am strong enough to meet him for a drink, have him come back to my home, and still not sleep with him."

Crazy talk! You have to get all of this chatter out of your head, and recognize there are several times in the healing process that you will have to remind yourself to be extra strong in your conviction that your breakup is for the best.

Step 3:

Make A Case For Stubbornness: Have A Head Like A Rock

In case you didn't know: In Italian, "Fungol" is a bad word. "Stubborn" isn't. Quite the contrary, an Italian American who is stubborn probably has something to be proud of.

Italian American men, like those in the Russo family, have heads like rocks. The women are tough cookies too! We aren't the only ones. There must be something in Italian American blood. No matter our gender, or who is in our family of origin, when we "Eyetalian" Americans get attached to an idea, don't try to convince us otherwise! For the most part, nothing you say or do will change the mind of a truly stubborn Italian American, because we secretly *like* to be stubborn. If you try to engage us in a verbal sparring match, you might as well just back down now, because you aren't going to win. We are always right—even when we are wrong. That's just the way it is. So as my mother would say, "Put that in your pipe and smoke it."

Two Types of People in The World

Without a doubt, there are two breeds: Italians and those who want to *be* Italian!

Allow me to enlighten you about Italian American pride. Let's start with the motherland. Italy is a country to be proud of—one known for beautiful countryside, coast, and ancient cities with marble columns and amazing architecture. When people think of Italy, they think of Roman mythology, gorgeous language, literature, renowned art, music, history, grapevines, World Cup wins, and the most delicious food money can buy. They think of the greats like Michaelangelo, Da Vinci, and all the other beautiful Italians who accomplished so much while managing to look so sophisticated. Italians aren't just great and fabulous dressers in the magical place that is Italy. They are great (and stylish) in the United States too. In fact, the millions of Italians who have migrated to the United States over the last two centuries have played a tremendous role in American history.

The pioneering Italian Americans accomplished lots when they came over to Ellis Island and have been truly proud of their ability to create something from nothing. Without a doubt, we are a special group of people who made astonishing achievements in many disciplines. From Renaissance art, to architecture, to philosophy, literature, science, and medicine, there are many reasons for our pride. There are so many Italian Americans who made a wide range of contributions in film, music, and sports, influencing the U.S. in an unforgettable way. There is Marlon Brando, Nicholas Cage, Sylvester Stallone, Susan Sarandon, Al Pacino, Robert De Niro, and Martin Socorcese. There is Joe Montana, Vince Lombardi, and Yogi Berra. There's Frank Sinatra, Tony Bennet, Dean Martin, John Bon Jovi, Bruce Springsteen, Liza Minnelli, and Madonna. There are Pulitzer Prizes that went to Italian Americans, The Bank Of America, former NYC Mayor, Rudy Giuliani, the development of Catholicism in the America, and, of course, Gianni Versace. I could go on and on. How about the fact that every great city has a Little Italy? The Italian Americans have festivals like the famous San Gennaro that takes place in New York's Little Italy every September. New York Italians even celebrate in the outer boroughs too with the Feast of The Saints and the 18th Avenue Feast in Brooklyn. They surely don't need just a single occasion to celebrate.

As Italian Americans, we show our pride on a regular basis with the clothes we wear, the bumper stickers on our car, the flags we display, and even the online chat rooms we've frequented. (Come on, if you were thirteen or older and living in the NY/NJ/CT area in 1997 with an internet connection, you know you've heard of the AOL chat room, "Italian Hotties"!) Indeed, Italian Americans love to share recipes, stories, and photographs. They pass them down from one generation to the next. And if they are as Italian American and proud as I am, they even Tweet the world photos of the Jersey Italian Gravy they had for Sunday dinner.

Clearly, being stubborn or "too proud" has treated we Italian Americans well when it has meant being focused on our goals. Think of it this way: When you hate to be wrong, you fight to prove yourself right. This type of tunnel vision can help you get what you want too, and you don't even have to be DaVinci! I bet you've already exercised some of this Italian American stubbornness in your life. Consider how you may have applied such focus to your career, for instance. If you are genuinely happy and successful in your career, you probably took a ton of steps to get where you are today.

You went to school. Took notes in class. Studied for tests. Wrote research papers at 2 a.m. Passed midterms and finals.

You created a resume. Drafted cover letters. Applied for jobs. Awkwardly introduced yourself to strangers wearing name tags at networking events.

You made it past the gatekeeper. Got the interview. Landed the job. Negotiated the salary.

You even got health insurance. *Maybe.*

You started your career. You worked your way to the top of the corporate ladder. Or you became an entrepreneur and gave your blood, sweat, and tears. You made a life. Found your passion.

Of course you got to where you are today because you worked hard, but also because you were stubborn. You wouldn't settle for any run-of-the-mill-job. Your determination fueled you to take the action you needed to get you what you wanted.

You did all of these things because you were stuck on the idea that you wanted to have the career of your choice. If you have to put this much effort into your career in order to succeed, why would you be able to put any less into your relationship and expect it to be successful?

Likewise, a hard head can really help you when dealing with something like the process of healing from a breakup, because you need something to get you through the challenges. (By the way, throwing yourself into your career is one of the best distractions!) As you gather by now, getting over an ex is not like making instant oatmeal or even steel cut oats. It is more like a measure of all the effort it takes to make eggplant lasagna with sauce from scratch, multiplied by one thousand. It is something that you will have to work at and struggle with each and every day until your heart is healed.

At times, you will feel like you have a disease because you can't stop thinking about your ex. You will be convinced there is something terribly wrong with you. Others may suggest your behavior is abnormal, just because they've never met anyone who has loved as hard as you. Love messes with your mind, as you will rationalize that if you want to be with your ex this badly that maybe the two of you are meant to be together. See you *can* be stubborn.

If you want to heal, you are going to have to make like a stubborn Italian American and never waver in your belief that your breakup is for the best. Instead of being too stubborn to let go of all the history, memories, time, and effort you put in with your ex, you need to be stubborn about other things--like not settling for less than what you deserve.

You Don't Need That Shit

If you didn't settle for any old job, you shouldn't settle for any old relationship. You should be way too proud to go back to your ex. Ideally, you'd be just as proud as the Italian American bella who'd tell a stunad to "go eff himself" and believe it with every fiber of her being! I know your ex and the breakup may have messed with your self-esteem, and that consequently, you may not be super-confident. Whatevs. You can "fake it 'til ya make it". **But do realize that you will not actually make it unless you can get yourself on the path of being one hundred percent convinced that your relationship can't be fixed.**

Furthermore, it would be ideal if you could be super stubborn in the belief that it isn't *worth* being fixed.

You might say that you wouldn't settle for less than what you deserve but still consider going back to see if you can get something better out of it. Going back would be settling, because the relationship is broken. At the point in which your relationship became damaged enough for a breakup to occur, it became clear that one or both of you did not have your whole heart in it. Therefore, you wouldn't be returning to a healthy love, you would be returning to something comfortable, but broken. In this case, getting back with your ex would look no better than two people who are just going through the motions. Who needs *that* shit? It wouldn't be anymore satisfying to you than life is to the people who are just trying to keep up with The Joneses, The Kardashians, or whichever family on their block makes them think "the grass is greener" on the other side of their house--or TV.

If you truly believe everything we've covered-namely that your ex is a stunad, that you deserve better, and that your relationship could not be fixed-you are well on your road to recovery. Your biggest focus should be on sticking to your guns! Never stop reminding yourself that you always need to be prepared for those certain circumstances in life that can test your belief, blur your judgment, and make you think reaching out to your ex is a good decision.

One time when you really need to be one stubborn biatch is during the holidays. Without a doubt, lots of people have a love-hate relationship with the holidays. From the colored lights, baked goods, bows, and holly comes everything to the stress of gift-giving and family drama, to the lethargy from overindulgence in food and drinks. Then, of course, there is the stress of those who don't love their love lives.

Holiday Survival Tips

If you are newly single-or have been in the past during the holidays-you may be familiar with the anxiety that comes from having to find a halfway decent date for the office party. If so, don't indulge in self-pity and sulking out of loneliness because this is yet another holiday season without any prospects to kiss under the mistletoe. No one likes to be alone during the holidays, but being single at this time isn't a reason to creep into an ex's bedroom at 3 a.m. or settle for the random hookup at the bar. Instead, it is a time to reconnect with friends, family, and all those other people you ignored when you were with your ex. Find a new way to make the holidays special.

A word of advice: As you strive to find new meaning during the holidays, don't beat yourself up if you are feeling weak for your ex during this season. It is common for people start looking in the rear view mirror when they are flying solo at "the most wonderful time of the year". They start getting lonely then-or around Valentine's Day-and find themselves reminiscing about a past love relationship. They start thinking of past holidays spent with an ex, remembering those occasions as much better than they actually were. They do this for birthdays and anniversaries as well—remembering what they bought their ex, what gift they received, and exactly what each celebration entailed.

If you ever question whether to call an ex to say Happy Thanksgiving, Merry Christmas, or Happy Birthday, my answer is the same no matter what the occasion. It is NOT necessary. Sure, it's nice, but so is feeding the needy at a soup kitchen. (It'd also be nice if they had fried zeppoles there!) If you must get in touch in some way, an email or text would be better. A card could work as long as you -nor your ex or your ex's new partner- mistake it for an open invitation to communicate regularly.

If you feel strongly about contacting an ex on a holiday, your goal should be to avoid awkwardness and extended conversation. Don't even think about gifts or grand gestures. Before you even get in touch, you should ask yourself *why* you want to do it. Is it *really* to wish the ex a happy birthday or were you hoping you could get together, celebrate, and fall magically into bed? If you are trying to reconnect romantically, you really don't need to go there. Remember, you are making like a stubborn Italian American who is trying to create a new future, and you cannot do that by clinging to the past.

Another time you need to make a case for stubbornness is when you are feeling down and out. Life can be very difficult, and it is even more so when you don't have a partner to get you through the rough patches. If you were used to relying on your ex for emotional support you may feel like you can't get through certain circumstances without his or her shoulder to cry on. Hell, you may even feel sad that you don't have a shoulder to lean on when you are using public transportation. (That's how I felt post-breakup when I saw all those girls on the 6 train with their head on their boyfriend's shoulder. On one hand, I wondered: What is it about being in a relationship that makes a woman unable to keep her head in an upright position? I mean, is she really that tired? On the other hand, it looks appealing. *Shit. I want someone's shoulder to lean on too. And, by the way, how does she have a boyfriend? Eww. I'm prettier than her!*) Every single man or woman who really wants a relationship has moments of weakness in which their mind goes back to an ex.

Fantasy vs. Reality

It is only natural to recall memories of an ex and yearn for the good feelings he or she had brought into your life during tough times. If you failed a test or got fired from a job, your ex would be the one that you called. If your family member got sick, your ex would be the first one to come to the hospital with you. If you get sick now, you may be even more likely to miss your ex. When you are laying in bed high on cough syrup, your mind can take you to some crazy places. You may start feeling sorry for yourself and thinking about how life would be so much better with your ex. News flash: This is a fantasy. In fact, maybe it's even a fantasy that your ex did all those nice things for you. When you are experiencing pain, you are even more likely to paint a picture of memories that were much better than the reality of the experiences you had with your ex.

Just take any feelings of longing for what they are: You craving the person who was previously your source of comfort. I guarantee if you were to see your ex again, it wouldn't be long before you realize that your fantasy is much better than the reality of who your ex is.

But get it through your thick head: You should not see your ex at this time. (Really. Please be stubborn about this!) You have to force yourself to remember everything bad with your ex so you can focus on being stubborn in your belief that your breakup is a positive thing. You have to convince yourself that you can tap into other sources of comfort. Your friends and family can bring you chicken soup when you are sick too, you know. They can even go yell at your neighbors when you can't get any sleep because they are making football-watching-orgasm-sounds that are audible from your apartment. There are many times you are going to be tired in life, so you should learn to self-soothe. When you are riding the subway for instance, you can remind yourself that you don't have to be like the girl who is resting her head on a man's shoulder. There are tons of happy singles that are perfectly capable of holding their own head up while riding public transportation, thank you very much. You can learn to be one of them!

Lastly, you need to get your stubborn on when you are faced with the temptation of sex with the ex. Note: Sex is ABSOLUTELY out of the question.

When you are tempted to sex your ex, ask yourself this: What are all the ways that sex with your ex is like exposing yourself to damaged goods? *Helllllo, the glass is broken. Do want to leave the broken glass alone or try to put it back together and risk getting cut by the pieces?* Sex with your ex can cut you. It can also give you STDs, yeast infections, parasites, and unwanted children. Sex with someone you share a lot of history with can mess with your mind. It can feel both familiar and strange at the same time. It can throw any progress you made in moving on from your ex right out the window. Blame it all on that "cuddle hormone," also known as oxytocin, for bonding you to your stunad ex in the first place! If you have sex with your ex now, it can make you think you and your ex should get back together.

Plus, you can mistake a pleasurable romp between the sheets for real intimacy. If you want to get back together afterward and your ex does not, it can lead to even more hurt and rejection. What is more painfully embarrassing than that? Sadly, it could be worse if you continue to have sex and proceed with the relationship. If you rush back into a relationship before you or your ex have changed, there is a likelihood of plenty more pain. Sex doesn't fix a broken relationship. It just puts a band aid on it, but the scars are still there.

Whether you have just one hookup up or continue sexing your ex, if the sex is no longer good, it can actually be quite depressing, as you may realize what you had with your ex is gone. It may make you think back to times when things were better between you and your ex and wish you could bring them back. It can make you feel insecure. It can be awkward to look your ex in the eye while feeling so exposed--awkward enough to make you want to cry. If your ex is no longer looking you in the eye, it can feel even worse. You may wonder what he or she is thinking and if they've been with others since you've broken up. You won't be able to stop obsessing about this. ("Were the others better in bed?" "And, OMG, did they use protection?") If you are one of the few lucky freaks in the world who has no insecurities about your body or sexual performance, you may start to develop such insecurities at this time. (Yeah, you can thank your ex for that.) On top of all this, you have the potential to feel very empty. A sexual experience with an ex is something one, or both of you, may come to regret. Who really wants an ex running around with a chip on his or her shoulder bragging about having boned you?

Let's be honest: Despite all you now know about why having sex with your ex can do more harm than good, I realize you are human and therefore flawed. So you may still want to sleep with your ex. Don't worry, you would never be this crazy if you hadn't fell for you ex. No one is really that crazy until they loved the person who made them crazy.

If you are contemplating sex, you are clearly scoring high on the crazy-ometer, and it is a good idea to protect yourself. A handy list of all the things you'd be better off doing instead of "doing it" with your ex can offer more protection than a condom!

So I beg you to go create your list! If you are really feeling the need to be sexual, find an outlet other than your ex. It doesn't have to be watching porn or hooking up with a random stranger at a bar. You could browse profiles on online dating sites just to show yourself there are people out there who you could get cozy with in the future! I suggest most of the ideas on your list are nonsexual, because right now your brain associates your sexuality with your ex. You will get away from that in time if you focus on other activities.

Here are some ideas to start you off:

- Call a friend-preferably one who hates your ex-and chat all night

- Cook up a really good, gourmet meal or just order in

- Clean your place like it is your job while blasting uplifting music

- Pump iron at the gym

- Take a class on a subject you have always wanted to learn more about

- Attend a workshop, lecture, or event in your city or a city near you

- Read a trashy romance novel or watch a romantic comedy

- Take a sex-themed exercise class like striptease, pole dancing, or belly dancing

- Go shopping for sexy lingerie, a new outfit, or umm, sex toys

- Organize a Girls or Boys Night Out

- Find a cause that speaks to you and volunteer through a charity

- Get a massage at a highly rated spa you have never been to

When you are bored, lonely, and on the verge of abandoning your stubbornness, remember that the possibilities for how you could put your time to good use are endless.

Action Steps to Make a Case for Stubbornness and Have a Head Like a Rock

Recognize all of your strengths and take pride in them.

Chances are, there is a lot about you that is really great! There are many reasons to have gratitude in your life, and a lot of the good things that have happened in your past relationship are the result of your goodness. Write them down in your journal. Give yourself a shot of confidence as you fully recognize you are a person of value. When you know your worth, you will realize that you don't have to put up with the bullshit you did when you were with your ex.

If you aren't feeling pride about who you are and where you are in life, just start pretending you are for a little bit of time every day. You should give this a try, because it works. (And smiling really does make you happier, too!) You eventually have to figure out who you really are and become proud of everything about yourself. Your success in life depends on it! Those who know who they are attract positive people and positive experiences into their lives.

Get in touch with your stubborn side.

Grab a pen and make another list. Go deep and reflect on your life. Think of all the ways you benefited or could have benefited from being stubborn throughout the years. Do you see that if you are stubborn enough, you can get everything and anything you want from the boardroom to the bedroom? Consider how things could have been better in your past relationship if you were more stubborn. Where did you need to put your foot down like an Italian American would? Where did you need to draw your line in the sand?

Always remind yourself why you should get over your ex.

Grab a piece of paper. Copy down the following and fill in these blanks. Put this up on your refrigerator, bathroom mirror, bedroom door, or wherever you will see it daily.

My ex is a ________________. (Insert profanity)

What my ex did to me
was____.
(i.e. disrespectful, rude, insensitive, inexcusable, etc)

I am so much better without my ex because
____.

I deserve a
____

____.

Step 4:

Stay Up & Fight-- For A Healthy (Single)Life

Since we Italian Americans are so stubborn, it should come as no surprise that we are fighters who are willing to do whatever it takes to get what we truly want.

However, Americans of other ethnicities may not perceive us that way at a first glance.

When people think of Italian culture, they may think of laid-back Europeans going with the flow of life. They may think of people lingering around outdoor cafes, sipping glasses of wine during long work day breaks. It is true the Italians know how to relax, but they also know how to work hard—despite the sad state of the economy in Italy today. Of course, times were much tougher in Italy back in the nineteenth and twentieth centuries. Italians came to the United States to escape the intolerable conditions. They worked even harder to get ahead in life back then.

When the first groups of "off the boat" Italians came to the U.S., they didn't have it easy. They left everything familiar for this foreign land with nothing more than a prayer and the hope of scoring a cramped tenant apartment. They were tired, poor, and without any education or clue as to how things would work out. They'd not only have to find a home, but learn a new language, and get a job. Being that most came without all of their family members, they knew they'd have to send a lot of their income home. They shared space to save money, and they faced discrimination for being immigrants as well as for being Catholic. They were risk takers indeed, sacrificing their health, youth, comfort, and dreams for a better life for their families.

From Italy, there came many hard workers. There were the laborers from the Southern cities with little formal education, people who worked on the railroads and in sweat factories, and those who made pennies shoveling, building, and sewing. Although it took them time develop greatness due to the incredible hardships they faced, they were strong and ready to fight for success. Ultimately, they had what it took to win.

My point? If you are willing to put in the amount of effort these Italian Americans did in order to get over your ex, I am sure you can be successful too.

To reiterate, you must first acknowledge that you are in an unhealthy and unhappy state. I don't want to further depress you, but being healthy is not an easy task post- breakup, especially if you just walked away from a toxic relationship. People who have experienced conflict, traumatic events, or any form of emotional, sexual, or physical abuse within a relationship really suffer. If you were in a toxic relationship, you probably won't fully realize the toll it took on your self-esteem and overall life satisfaction until long after you leave it. **It is only when you can admit that you have been wronged and damaged in some way that you can begin to make progress in your recovery.** It is only then that you can decide to fight with all you've got like an Italian American would.

You should want to fight hard, because what could be more important than your health and happiness? You've heard it before: You have to love yourself before you can truly love anyone else. How could you love anyone if you are not comfortable in your own skin as a single? You can't! You are going to have to acknowledge that you are lonely and uncomfortable being single. If this is not true, you can skip the next few paragraphs and pat yourself on the back.

If you are unsure if you qualify as a lonely, uncomfortable single, try taking yourself out for a solo meal at a restaurant.

When you are sitting alone in a restaurant feeling self-conscious that you don't have a plus one, your heartache can really hit you--especially if you are out on Date Night. Don't lash out at the waiter taking away the place setting after asking "Is anyone joining you tonight?" *Eh.* I know you'll want to be like: "Thanks for the reminder, buddy, that it's just me, myself, and I." It is not his fault that you are sad to notice the groups of friends laughing, reminding you of the good times you shared with your friends pre-breakup-- before you became officially no fun to hangout with. It's not his fault that you'll see couples gazing into each others eyes reminding you of better times with your ex or families with cute babies reminding you of your aborted dream of having a child. Instead of looking at being out alone as the worst thing that ever happened to you, get to a place where your mind is calm and you can not only get through it, but enjoy it!

Do realize that in the early days of your transition to the single life, you will find yourself thinking about things quite differently than you used to--especially when you are out and about on your own. Instead of wondering which bottle of wine a significant other would most like to share at the restaurant, you will wonder if the other customers will look at you funny if you order wine with your meal. A glass of red after a long work week on Friday seems like it might be acceptable enough. But having a second? *Hmmm.* At best, some stuffy khakis-wearing-couple-from-Connecticut might suspect you go heavy on the booze. At worst, the second glass might ignite the water works--i.e. the tears that come from thinking of your ex while intoxicated. And if the bruschetta is not enough, can your order a second appetizer? Or would that make the waiter think you are emotional eating? Such questions-and the discomfort in finding the answers- may seem challenging in the moment, but the answer is simple. In sum, you should just do what you want!

If you wish to mend a broken heart Italian American style, you cannot deprive yourself of any satisfaction just because you are single. If "a real Italian" was hungry after hours of work and was far from home, he or she would not think twice about stopping in a restaurant for a great meal. It is only the Americanist of Americans who would sacrifice quality of dining experience for not feeling judged by strangers. Their European counterparts would not choose a sub par panini at a crowded

Starbucks just because eating alone seems more acceptable in such a casual place.

Someone who connects with Italian culture is going to choose the trendy corner restaurant with exposed brick, hardwood floors, soft music playing, roses on the bar, and candles on the tables. The question of whether to wine and dine has only one answer for the real Italians and Italian Americans. YES! Those true to the culture will drink that wine front and center with their head held high. I've been there. Can you take yourself there too? If not, you have a bit of a way to go before you can have a healthy single life.

Single & Loving It

Don't get discouraged about your single status. Contrary to the popular belief of some, you could even grow to love the perks of being single! In case you are wondering how you will ever survive and be happy now that you are minus your plus one, embrace this fact: Being in a relationship doesn't guarantee happiness, and being single does not equal unhappiness. Having a happy single lifestyle is crucial to your success in getting over your ex. Convince yourself that being single isn't so bad, and that it is better than being with your ex. There are lots of benefits of being single--beyond just not having to answer to anyone, shave off body hair, or buy presents for anyone's family but your own. Being alone can prove to be a tremendous learning experience. As time goes on, you will discover all sorts of interesting tidbits about yourself, and you'll become more intimately acquainted with you.

Understanding your personality better and standing strong on your own two feet will really help you in love and life. Embrace this new opportunity to find out more about who you are. Realize that in some way, your ex was stifling who you are and what you stand for; this is, in part, why your relationship didn't work out. Identify all of the new things you love about being single, or in other words, recognize all the things you hated about being with your ex! If you get excited about being single, you will be able to embrace a healthy life.

Society tends to stigmatize being single, as marriage is an institution that has historically been considered beneficial for humanity. Since most people end up getting married, being single is not the norm. If you are less than enthused about being in the unattached minority, I understand. Sometimes people ask me if I am single like it is a crime not to be married--even in New York City where many people get married years after they hit my ripe old age of 30. Of course I get judged a little more harshly than the average girl being that I've built a name for myself as a dating and relationship expert, but I know a lot of you who are on your own get it too! If you are like me, you probably want to lead a full life, have success in your career, and keep up with your friends, family, and social calendar. You probably want to be in a relationship, but only the right relationship. You may know that being single is like being in the meantime. (In other words, it won't last forever.) You probably want to have as much fun as you can in the time that you aren't working hard to achieve your personal and professional goals. When you naturally get a little lonely and miss an ex or two, you could think your single status is much worse than it really is. You could feel like the fifth wheel when invited out with friends or notice you are barely getting invitations if all your friends are coupled up. You could think it is more expensive to live a single life being that your taxes are higher and you have no one to split the bills with. You may even come to believe that the world is made for couples!

Just as these thoughts are counterproductive, there are certain behaviors that can sabotage your recovery. I've touched on many of them already. But it is so important that you avoid these common post-breakup temptations, that they bear repeating. DO NOT:

- Do nothing but sleep and cry

- Allow your sorrow take a physical toll on your body--giving you cold and flu-like symptoms, dark under eye circles, weight loss, hair loss, acne, Irritable Bowel Syndrome, etc.

- Engage in emotional eating to the point where you are gaining weight and getting even more depressed

- Feel insecure about yourself almost all of the time

- Torture yourself over the thought of your ex marrying, having babies, and living happily ever after with someone else

- Develop anxiety about going to places where you have memories with your ex

- Talk about your ex too much--which can traumatize you again

- Be delusional enough to wait for your ex when your ex isn't looking back

As if all that isn't hard enough, there is always the possibility of that one instance that could test of your strength like nothing else. It is, of course, the random encounter with your ex.

The Ex Encounter: Because You Can't Always Live In An Ex-Free Zone

The post-breakup story goes something like this: After weeks of seeing no one besides the delivery boys who come to your apartment with a fix of emotional eats, your friends finally convince you it is time to leave the nest. You start getting dressed up, going out, and hoping to meet some singles. One night, it happens, and everyone's nightmare becomes your reality. You meet the last person on earth you'd want to meet--your ex.

Before you start freaking out and lead yourself to a full-on panic attack, rest assured that there are other responses besides crawling into a hole in and dying. You may not achieve your dream of a world where you'd never have to run into an ex, but you could find some peace of mind by remembering some simple survival tactics. The first run-in is the hardest, and if it happens again, you'll be a pro if you just obey the rules that follow.

Don't approach your ex: Just do not go up to him or her first. This may sound silly, but remember you are doing this Italian American style, and

Italian Americans are way too proud to make the first move. Neither of you were expecting this random encounter, and you can't be quite sure how your ex will react. If your ex wants to chat with you, he or she will come up to you and start a friendly conversation. Allow him or her to ask questions. You can ask follow-up questions of a similar nature, but don't initiate the questions. If your ex just wants to say hi and get out of there as quickly as possible, he or she will keep it brief and run away. Just let it be, and you will feel better than you would if you initiated conversation that didn't turn out well. Save yourself the embarrassment.

Don't let 'em see you sweat: Clearly, you are sweating. You thought you were safe and in an ex-free zone. Life just threw you a curveball, and the best choice is to put on your game face and play. You can act a little surprised to see your ex. That is, of course, better than giving him or her the impression that you were expecting such a run-in. Just keep it casual. Say something lighthearted and fun like "Oh, wow, what a surprise. Didn't expect to see you here." The important thing is that you act nonchalant, like running into him or her is no big deal. Even if you are on the verge of tears, you have to keep it together. Channel that Italian American pride! Remember, you are too good to be anything but strong in front of your ex!

Make a great impression: You want your ex to walk away thinking that you look better than ever and seem like you are doing well. Since you didn't have time to coordinate the perfect- running-into-your-ex-outfit, you are just going to have to muster up all the confidence you can. For future reference: Take this chance encounter as evidence that fashion consultant and media personality. Tim Gunn, is a genius. As he famously said, "If you wouldn't want to run into your ex in it, don't wear it." In the meantime, communicate your boldness and positive energy with your body language. Make sure you sound graceful too. When your ex asks how you are, keep in mind "I'm doing fine" will not suffice. Share specific details to communicate the idea that you are doing well without your ex. Make sure you briefly highlight some new and exciting happenings in your life in an honest way. You can exaggerate just as you would pad your resume, but don't lie. Your ex knows who you are inside and out, so be yourself. By yourself, I mean a better version of the self that you were when with your ex.

Keep Calm And Carry On: As the British post-war saying goes, don't let anything ruffle you. You must maintain a calm demeanor and move forward. Your goal is to survive this ex encounter with as much elegance and grace as possible. It *can* be done, but there may be some challenges along the way. Maybe just seeing your ex makes you want to get back together or has you feeling very awkward. Don't worry, you probably don't look as awkward as you feel. Maybe your ex is trying to win this running-into-an-ex-game too.

Maybe your ex does something to upset you like, say, bringing up someone he or she is currently dating. Even worse, your ex might actually be there with another love interest. Don't worry. You aren't approaching. Don't go out of your way with any fake-friendliness if you aren't feeling the love. You are at wherever you ran into your ex for a purpose other than seeing your ex. So say your hello, say your goodbye, and get on with it. No sweat.

If you get through an awkward encounter with your ex, you deserve a jar of Nutella and maybe even a medal. You can breathe deeper after the horror is over, but you won't be off the hook for quite some time. In the initial phases of getting over an ex, there will be many things that will be a constant fight.

Here are ten obstacles you are going to have to get through to live a healthy, single life:

1. *The sadness:* There will be days when all you can write in your journal is: "Dear _____, I am so sad. I miss you so much. I think about you every day and sometimes I just burst into tears." So be it. When you are down, you need to pick yourself back up again. Tomorrow is a new day. Maybe you'll have something else to write then.

2. *The desire to prove your awesomeness to your ex:* When everyone sees your greatness except the one person you really want to, it is super

annoying. But guess what? You don't need the approval of your ex--or anyone.

3. *The power of denial:* If you're single but your Facebook profile still says you are in a relationship, you need to accept your new reality.

4. *Loneliness*: This is the thing that happens at night when you realize you have no one to cuddle up with. It is inevitable. Try getting a body pillow or maybe even a dog.

5. *Missing everything about your ex:* It's really difficult when you are constantly reminded of all the reasons you miss your ex, but you really can find something else to think about.

6. *Feeling crazy:* After a breakup, you may start to feel unstable--like you are losing your mind. You can feel both hopeful and doubtful about your ex. Love, especially lost love, makes everyone a little crazy sometimes.

7. *Rejection:* Getting over someone not because you want to, but because you have to, is the worst. The pain of rejection can sting for a while. You and your ego are bruised.

8. *The urge to stalk:* If you are used to talking to someone on a regular basis and the communication comes to a halt, it is only natural that you want to find out what is going on. Constantly checking your ex's social media profiles and accounts or going to places he or she frequents just isn't good for your sanity.

9. *The What If's:* When a relationship that you really wanted to work fails, it's easy to go back and beat yourself up for doing things the way you did. You may constantly ask yourself : "What if I did x, y, or z, differently?" Well, newsflash, babycakes, you didn't, and you can't change the past. So, get over it!

10. *The False Hope:* Deep down, you may know your ex is not for you. Yet, there may be a little voice that says "Ya never know…" Realize

that voice is the voice of a stunad stuck in denial. Don't put your energy into someone that is never going to change.

So the question is: Are *you* ready to change? Are you ready stand up and fight?

Action Steps to Stay Up and Fight for a Healthy Single Lifestyle

Take care of your physical health.

The Italian Americans didn't come to this country to play around, and you too, must get really serious and commit to doing what is best for your recovery. You have to take care of your physical health if you want to have sound mental and emotional health.

Take someone who just had open heart surgery, for instance. When in recovery, patients are advised to make some serious lifestyle changes. Now I am not a doctor, but I do know that some of the standard medical advice which must be followed after such a serious surgery includes exercising, maintaining a heart-healthy diet, and reducing stress. All of this advice is helpful for dealing not only with recovery from the emotional nightmare known as post-open heart surgery, but with getting over a bad breakup.

Who wouldn't benefit from eating good food, releasing endorphins, and generally taking care of themselves? Without a doubt, when going through a breakup, you have to be kinder to yourself than ever before. You are going through A LOT! Being truly heartbroken is actually quite similar to being in recovery from open heart surgery. *Seriously, this is not a stretch.* There is sadness, anger, frustration, stress, anxiety, and a general sense of hopelessness--not to mention guilt and regret in both scenarios. If you find yourself in either situation, you will truly know what it's like to be on an emotional roller coaster.

Are you there now? Well, you have to take the right actions to get your self off the roller coaster. Stalking your ex on Instagram is not one of them. Getting a good night's sleep is.

Take care of your mental health.

There was a study reported in *Circulation: Journal of the American Heart Association,* that can give you a reason to ditch your job and take a mental health day when going through a breakup. This study was done to monitor the health of the brokenhearted who were suffering due to the death of a loved one. The research revealed that the psychological stress from the loss contributed to an increase of heart attack risk by twenty-one percent the day after the death of the loved one. Fortunately, the study showed that the risk of heart attack did decrease and return to normal levels within the month of the death. Yet for many, the stress is still present and likely to cause all kinds of ugly health problems. With grief responsible for increasing blood pressure and heart rate, the likelihood of a heart attack should not be brushed off. As if this weren't bad enough, habits typically associated with breakups such as not eating and not sleeping can also increase heart attack risk.

There is an implication for you here: In the days and weeks after your split, you must take excellent care of yourself. Clearly, heartbreak puts you in your most vulnerable state. In times like these, it is better just to acknowledge that you are hurting and should be doing the things that will eventually restore your health, rather than just trying in vain to find "a quick fix". You don't need to stress yourself out trying to make everything all better. High cortisol levels lead to heart attacks, too, you know.

Take care of your emotional health.

When you are feeling stressed from a breakup, an emotional outlet is essential. The relationship is over, but your feelings about it are not. While it is not healthy to be talking and obsessing over your ex many years later, as mentioned earlier, it is good to initially let all your emotions out. Whether you talk to a trusted friend or therapist, or write in a journal, just make sure you express yourself fully. Allow yourself to feel your feelings and be patient, as it will take time for them to go away or change their form. It is normal to miss your ex from time to time, to wonder "what if," and to wish things played out differently. You can't control how you feel, but you can control what you do with those feelings. Choose to engage in activities that will keep you in a positive frame of mind, and keep doing them until you are happily healed.

Don't forget, one of the best ways you can get in touch with all those crazy emotions is to write about how you feel. That's right, I think you can mend your heart with a simple pen and paper. It worked for me. I am not the only one who makes this bold claim, and even open heart surgery survivors agree! Steve Ludwig, author of *See You In CCU-A Lighthearted Tale Of My Open-Heart Surgery*, says:

"The emotional ups and downs one experiences during heart surgery recovery can be so extreme, that writing was my only outlet. It was easier for me to express my feelings to a piece of paper because even talking out loud would set me off in tears."

Feel the same way whenever someone says your ex's name, much?

Keeping a journal could be tremendous help in dealing with the loss of your ex. Purge yourself of all those messy emotions by first recognizing what they are. Do not self-edit. Just write. If you do this often enough, you'll really come to understand your feelings and get to a place of clarity. Hopefully all this talk of open heart surgery and heart attacks makes you realize that a broken heart is not to be taken lightly. You really do have to make like an Italian American to succeed in the fight for a healthy single life.

Step 5:

Have Sunday Dinner: Family, Friends, & Food

La Famila is of great significance in Italian American culture. Our family ties are usually quite close. We generally believe that "blood is thicker than water," but there are family friends who we are equally loyal to when they are brought in and regarded as aunts, uncles, and godparents. We put utmost importance on nurturing family bonds. For Italian Americans, family comes first. Even though our families tend to be large and inclusive of a bunch of loud-mouthed, strong personalities who are all up in our business, they are our family and we love them. We even fall in love with our spouse's family, thinking it is respectful to celebrate the people who are important to him or her. Thanks to the Italian American values of loyalty and respect, we often find ways to "be civil" with family despite everything from petty fights to major blowouts, hypocrisy, hard heads, and drama. Sometimes there are family cut offs, but we try to keep the peace in the family, because we value family time and want everyone capable of being in the same room at family functions. There are a lot of family get- togethers for Italian Americans, which typically involve everyone sitting around the table and enjoying meals. Hence, the birth of a tradition called Sunday Dinner.

In many Italian American families, Sunday afternoons are the time when the whole family regularly gets together to talk, eat, and thoroughly bask in the culinary pleasure that is a full course Italian meal. (This often takes places after mass--another important tradition for many Italian Americans.) When you are going through a breakup, you should embrace the fact that your family and friends can help in many ways. Just being in their presence can work wonders for the heartbroken, and is essential that you understand the importance of maintaining your relationships during a difficult time. One thing you should never underestimate as you mend your broken heart Italian American style is the power of food, family, and friends at Sunday Dinner. A lot of effort goes into a Sunday Dinner. In an Italian

American household, the kitchen is the place to be social, whether you are cooking or just eating. But it doesn't always just start there.

Many Italian Americans have gardens where they grow squash and peppers and a whole lot of tomatoes. Growing up, my Italian American neighbors had a sick garden, and they were always generous enough to give us some of their produce! (Note: That is "sick" in a good way.) Word on the street is my great grandfather even had a grapevine. (I don't think he was alone, as a lot of Italian Americans made homemade wine "back in the day"!) We Italian Americans don't just make a meal from our garden though. We visit fruit and veggie stores, the butcher shop, the fish man, and the baker. All this effort, before we even make the pasta *sauce*--not to be confused with gravy. No wonder food is love in the Italian American household!

Naturally, we are convinced that no food is better than our food, and that Italian food is the best cure for anything. When you are Italian American and heartbroken, you mangiare. In other words, you eat. The idea of food and eating is so tied in with the relationships of Italian Americans. For instance, step into the shoes of a young Italian American woman: She meets a guy she likes and he asks her out on a date. To eat. She meets the guy's family; they eat. She introduces him to her family; they eat. She goes out with a friend to spill the juicy details of her love life, and they eat. The guy breaks up with her, and she eats again. *Ice-cream. Clearly.* Italian Americans like to be around other people who understand the importance of food in their culture.

As an Italian American woman, I wouldn't even go on a second date with a guy who didn't share my love of food. (If you want evidence, check out my reality dating blog as Ms. New York of www.3six5dates.com. Within my ninety-two dates in one year experience, you'll read stories like the one in which I dumped a guy who wouldn't let me order an appetizer on a first date!) People say laughter is the best medicine, but I am pretty sure that a good quality meal has triple the healing power if it is shared with friends and family. The fact that comedy clubs never have good food just blows my mind.

Anyone want to jump on a joint-venture with me? But who needs a comedy club, when you've got a big crazy Italian family to make you laugh until your stomach hurts? You can substitute Greek, Jewish, Puerto Rican, Asian, or African American. If you want to be like an Italian American, just go to your family for support and food in your time of need. It doesn't even have to be on Sunday. In fact, my Grandma Alice used to have feasts with her mother, sisters, and friends on *Saturdays.*

Now, a word of caution before you buon appetito: I am not suggesting you develop an unhealthy relationship with food. *Do you really need another unhealthy relationship?* Food can be comforting, and it can heal. Satisfying your hunger is a basic need and can immediately make you feel better than anything else can in the short term. However, food alone can't solve your problems. It can also create problems if you make bad choices around food and eating. (As any Italian American knows, ordering a Chicken Parm sub from a diner does qualify as a bad decision.) You are what you eat. If you continuously eat junk, it will catch up to you. If you starve yourself with diets or binge and purge, you will abuse your body, mind, and soul. *Let food help and not harm you.* Choose delicious, nutritious whole foods, but do cheat every now and then to satisfy your palate. Your heart is hurting enough, my luvah, and the last thing you need is a growling stomach. So feed yourself with the best of food and drink your money can buy.

If you are going to make like an Italian American, there will be times you are definitely going to skip the kale and quinoa salad, fill your plate with carbs, and go back for seconds. You can be a healthy Italian American at your next meal.

Bonus: People are also less likely to judge you if you gain weight, just like during pregnancy. But don't overdo it: You may not pull off the pudge as well as Tony Soprano did. *Awww. R.I.P James Gandolfini. We love you.* Accept invites to dinner, and invite your people over for a home cooked meal if you are up to sharing the love. Hungry yet? Go make yourself a good meal, and enjoy it like an Italian American would.

Now, when you are done stuffing your face, I want you to think about the dynamics in Italian American families, so you can understand the ways certain relationships can help you get over your ex.

It is no secret that mothers are deeply respected as the pillar of the Italian American home. Old school Italian American families keep women in the housewife role where they do the cooking, cleaning, and child rearing. Mothers have close bonds with their daughters and prepare them to be "wife material" by showing them how to manage a household. Of course, this involves mothers spending a lot of time in the kitchen teaching their daughter(s) how to cook. Recently, I made eggplant lasagna with my mother for a holiday dinner and realized what a bonding experience this time consuming task can be. Yeah, you try frying the eggplant, making the cheese mix, boiling, layering, and saucing up all those noodles in less than 2.5 hours! *But, hey, I'm legit wife material now.* In more modern day Italian American families, the father is not the sole breadwinner. When Mama works outside the kitchen, the Italian American man will sometimes pick up some of the household chores—namely taking out the garbage. *Just kidding....kind of!* Some Italian American men do more than that. (Please keep in mind that I come from a family in which my father did not start making his own tea (by placing a tea bag in a mug of hot water) until I was in my twenties. He has since come a long way and is a bit more helpful around the house.) Whether old school or new age, nearly all Italian American families are sure to share the old school Italian value of respect for the mother.

In many families, the relationship between Italian American mothers and sons is particularly strong. No doubt, there are Mama's Boys. You can learn a lot about Italian American culture by looking at the relationship between an Italian American mother and her Mama's Boy. If you want to expedite your education, just watch *Jersey Shore's* Vinny Guadagnino interacting with his adorable, Italian mother. By the way, ladies and gay men, if you ever want to date an Italian American Mama's Boy like Vinny, you should know that the survival of your relationship depends on how well you mesh with his mother!

Let me break down the rules for you. (Do note that some of these rules may apply to men of other ethnic backgrounds as well.) Obviously, you aren't ready to date anyone new yet, but you will get there. As many who've found love will tell you, it can happen when you least expect it.

Just put the following rules in the back of your mind for now in case a Mama's Boy crosses your path in the near future:

1. *His mother is always right.* If you say she is wrong, you put him in the middle. If he has to chose, honey, his choice won't be you. After all, they go way back—to the womb! How can you compete with that?

2. *If you can't beat her, join her.* And you can't. This is one battle you aren't going to win, so you might as well play on the same team. Get on her good side and stay there. She has a lot of influence over her son.

3. *Shut your mouth and know your role.* Wow, I sound mean, huh? Well, that is exactly how you will sound to your man if you say anything bad about his mom. If you need to bitch, hire a therapist. *Or better yet, hire me.*

4. *Face the facts: Girls, you are going to have to do some typical "female things."* Don't forget that you better jump up to clear the table with his mama after Sunday dinner. You have to help with the dishes too–with a smile. If you don't do this, she will complain: "That girl doesn't lift a damn fingernail." Pick the lesser evil here. You can either load a dishwasher or have her chirping in his ear.

5. *Clearly, he is going to expect you to pamper him.* A lot of Italian American men are used to their mothers doing everything for them from laundry to preparing their meals–even when they are well into their 20's, 30's, 40's, and 50's. Actually, sometimes, it never stops. If you don't do these things-or at least arrange for them to be done-the extreme mama's boys will question your value as a girlfriend, wife, woman, or gay man.

6. *Her cooking is the best.* A mother's culinary skill is one of the main reasons a Mama's Boy doesn't leave home. It is not because they don't have the money to rent or buy a place of their own or because they can't drop off their button-downs at the dry cleaners. They stay because the woman who gave them life makes it too good for them to leave. The reality is: You are either going to have to learn to cook like his mother or watch him push your food around on his plate.

7. *Your sex life may resemble that of a teenager.* If he lives at home and the mama is really old school, you aren't going to have much privacy in the bedroom. You may have to sneak in and out of the house and keep the volume down when feeling frisky. You might have to hide naked in a closet if she walks in when you two are getting busy. And God forbid, you may have to leave the door open in your grown boyfriend's mama's home! This just comes with the territory. So does her buying his "underwears."

8. *She's not going anywhere.* The biggest challenge of dating a Mama's Boy is integrating her into your life on daily and weekly basis while maintaining a healthy boundary to protect your romantic relationship. There will be many phone calls, visits, and expectations. If you get married, realize you will be marrying your man and his mom.

Got all that?

Clearly, an Italian American mother plays a pretty important role in the family. If you want to adopt the values of this culture to heal your heart, you can not forget about Mama. She may just be your backbone in a time of need. Indeed, the bond between a mother and child-whether son or daughter-is like no other. It is often said that no one loves someone the way a mother does. You should lean on your mother post breakup and look to her for love, encouragement, and support. If you are her daughter, she will truly empathize with you--especially if you have just broken up with an Italian American guy. (Chances are, a suave and charming Casanova once broke her heart too.) If you are her son, she will put you up on a pedestal and tell you that the girl you were dating wasn't good enough for you--especially because she didn't lift a damn finger in the kitchen! If your mother is deceased or you are estranged, rely on someone else in your life who you see as a maternal figure. Whether a grandmother, aunt, big sister, or friend, there is strength in the girl power around you.

Now, as for the papas….

Italian American fathers are traditionally seen as the providers in the old school Italian American family. They are the glue that holds the family together by going out into the world and working hard to bring home the pancetta. When they return home after a hard day's work, they expect their wife to greet them and provide them with a home cooked meal. Sometimes the men can seem sexist and pig-headed, because, well, they are. In other instances, they are just the hardworking breadwinners who want to feel cared for and respected. They care a lot about their family too. The fathers can be extremely protective of their daughters--especially in their teen years in which they often joke about pulling out a shotgun when their daughter's prom date comes to pick her up at the house. (If not a shotgun, they at least try to scare the guy into complying with the 12am curfew.) Without a doubt, Italian American fathers can be seen as loving but very strict and controlling. They are the type who wait up worried sick if you are out late, happy to ground you for weeks. Think the type of dad who says things to their daughters like "It's my way or the highway". On one hand, this control is because the fathers think they are always right and are just doing what is best. On the other, they want to keep their daughters young, innocent, and away from the opposite sex for as long as possible. They are quick to point out that they know how young guys think, because they were one of them. As fathers, they have to take on the role of disciplinarian and be the voice of reason.

Italian American fathers have close bonds with their sons, too. They may be a little tougher with them than they are with their daughters. Sometimes, they favor the sons. (After all, they are the ones who will surely carry on the family name.) They may be a bit less complimentary, but they are, nonetheless, very proud of their juniors.

Yes, the sons are often named after their fathers and grandfathers. The fathers and sons start family businesses together. Sometimes you even see three generations of men working together--whether investing in real estate, doing construction and project management, working in sanitation, or owning butcher shops and pizzerias. *Okay, this sounds very cliché. They can own other types of businesses too, but these are the industries where many Italian Americans in the tri-state area (where I grew up) have made their mark!* Fathers often get into fights with their sons when they work together. Things get heated when one party feels the other isn't pulling his weight, but things often get resolved quickly between an Italian American father and son.

If you have any type of problem in your love life, make like the Italian Americans and get some paternal support. Old school Italian American-especially the men- don't believe in going to therapy, which they regard as telling their problems to a stranger. They believe they should be able to work out their problems themselves by talking it out. *Correction: Yelling it out.* They are all about "keeping it in the family" and see going outside for help as a weakness. Your father, as head of the household, would be just the person to speak to if you want to keep this Italian American tradition. Of course, another man who has been a father figure in your life can get the job done too. Father figures are an incredible source of wisdom. A father may not coddle you the way a mother would. He may not want to hear all of the details of the breakup, but he can give you some unbiased advice. Since many men can be less emotional and more objective, they can really help you heal post breakup. You are already experiencing enough emotions. If you want to see things from a more rational lens, go to your father. Chances are, he will tell it like it is.

If you need more help coming to terms with the true nature of your relationship, be Italian American in spirit and take advantage of the wisdom and comforts of the entire family. Don't hesitate to ask them for advice about mending your broken heart. Second opinions from your siblings can be very powerful in helping you get through life's challenges. You grew up with these people. Your brothers and sisters are your flesh and blood. Your cousins are your sisters and brothers from another mother. They are very important in Italian American families, and they should be to you too. When I think of my sister Chrissy or my cousin Allison, I see why their insight about me is often on point: They are close to my age and understand truths about me that even my parents can't at a first glance, because they are of my generation and experienced my parents in the ways that I have. They will be able to relate to you and the issues you face, as they are your cohort dealing with the same challenges of modern day dating and relationships. You will fight with them, but they will be there for you no matter what if you let them. Aunts and uncles can offer a lot of support too. Sometimes, being that they aren't your parent, they can be even a little more objective with their advice, because they are a little farther away from the problem. *Shout out to my AJ!* They are also great confidants if you don't want to go there with your father or mother!

When your friends are like family, it is only natural that you go to them for advice too. They've known your history and if they are like the old school Italian-Americans guys who give their friends embarrassing nicknames, they have seen not only the good but the bad and ugly. (You know there's a story behind the birth of "Fat Tony"!) If your heart is hurting, lean on everyone you can trust to be there for you.

You can also seek support from those of a generation even farther from yours--your grandparents. Nonna and Poppa are the heart of the Italian American family and often live with or near the nuclear family. In their old age, they are generally only "put in a home" as a last resort if they need medical care that the family can't provide for them. They stick around and are very much part of the family dynamic. They love their grandchildren, give them advice, money, and support, as well as act as a buffer between the kids and parents. Italian American grandparents influence their grandchildren from their diaper-wearing days when they pinched their cheeks all the way through adulthood. Your grandparents have definitely been around the block, so make sure you take advantage of their experience.

Whether the people you call your family are your blood or friends that are like adopted family, you would be wise to get the support of as many of them as you can. In cahoots with the Italian American tradition, let your family baby and pamper you in your time of need. Of course, all families are different, but you can expect that, for the most part, they will take you in with open arms and embrace you. They will let you cry--to a point. They will encourage it for a while but will soon think enough is enough. At that point, you will just have to find new friends and family members to tell your saga to....

A word of advice: Go easy on your friends and family. I once did a survey in which my participants thought their famiglias didn't give particularly helpful advice post breakup--yet fifty percent of them said the best way for both men and women to get over a breakup is to get support from friends and family. According to my research, family and friends tend to say uninspiring things like the old:

"Everything happens for a reason."

"He wasn't good enough."

"You'll find someone better."

"It is for the best."

"She was wrong for you."

And the cringe-worthy...........

"I told you so."

Jeez, you'd think they could pull out a more motivational quote at a time like this. Perhaps, something from The Dalai Lama would work. He did say:

"Remember that not getting what you want is sometimes a wonderful stroke of luck."

True story; but scratch that. There is going to be a period of time where virtually no one will be able to say anything that fully makes you feel better. *Not even The Dalai Lama.* Less than stellar advice is no reason to turn your back to the support of your family and friends. You will benefit from just having social interaction with familiar faces. After heartbreak, you may find that you no longer trust as easily as you did before. It is like people will have to prove themselves once or twice now. (You will just be so fearful of dating someone that is like your stunad ex and having to deal with another breakup.) It helps to be surrounded by close friends and family, because they remind you there are people you can trust. If going back to your hometown or your parents' home is just a painful reminder of your ex, try seeing your family in a different context. You don't have to move across the country to run away from your problems, but a vacation with your family may do the trick.

Even locally, your family and friends can provide you with a change of surroundings when everything reminds you of your ex. When you want to call your ex, you can call and talk to them. They can talk some sense into you and show you that you don't have to endure the unnecessary pain of your ex.

Additionally, family helps you think clearly enough to see the situation with your ex for what it really was. Providing they know some of what went on in the relationship, they can help you by keeping you in reality. They will be the ones who get you to admit that you are in denial. It can be hard to come to terms with the notion that your ex shouldn't be put up on a pedestal--especially when you keep remembering all the good times. Your family will remind you of all the bad qualities of your ex. Their advice may be skewed, as they may have heard mostly negative things about your ex. They won't know all your delicious private moments and your ex's redeeming qualities, but right now that is ideal. You don't want to focus too much on the positive aspects of your past relationship. You do want to surround yourself with people who think your ex is a stunad, a strunz, or at the very least, not the right match for you. If your family thinks getting back with your ex would not only be a disgrace to you but to the entire family, your prognosis is looking even better!

Actions Steps To Have Sunday Dinner: Enjoy Family, Friends, And Food

Confide in your family and friends.

When the Italians came to the United States, they mingled with those of other ethnic groups, since they are such warm people. They were excellent networkers and formed unions and professional organizations. While they did business with others, many liked to "stick to their own kind," not because they were skeptical of others, but because they loved being around their own peeps. If you have a large network of friends and a big family, it will be easier to find people who care about you. Open up to them. Tell them what you are going through. Let them be a listening ear and a shoulder to cry on.

Ask for honest feedback.

It is only with family and close friends that Italian Americans "get real". The old school people don't believe in saying anything bad about family members to outsiders. It is considered a sign of disrespect and a breach of family loyalty. Some more modern day Italian Americans may slip up and say something negative about a family member to an acquaintance, but that person better not reciprocate with a negative comment.

If an outsider initiates a negative conversation about a family member, he or she better WATCH IT. Such opinions are considered offensive and unwelcome. It may seem hypocritical, but it totally makes sense to me. If you are in an Italian American family, the only people who are allowed to say something bad about you are those in your family. (FYI: I am very true to my Italian American roots in the sense that I would be very unapologetic for my actions towards anyone who offends my family. I tend to keep it classy and know that two wrongs don't make a right, but I am not afraid to let the offending party feel my wrath!)

Anyway, post-breakup is the time to ask for the cold, hard truth. Your family may sugarcoat it a little-even if they are straightforward Italian Americans- because they will be uncertain whether or not you can handle it. Make sure you see the iron fist behind the velvet glove, and realize that they are giving you tough love beneath that exterior. Ask them to tell you what they really thought of your relationship and figure out how the new information they provide can help you move on.

Eat well.

Most Italian Americans never want to be anything other than Italian American. Clearly this has much to do with the power of pasta and Prosecco with their paesanos! Now is the time for you to get in touch with your own pride and the people that you care about over a meal. Sunday Dinner is magical, and instead of eating alone, you should do it up Italian American style with your family and friends on the regular. If you can't cook a six course meal at home, just get some of it catered. *I won't tell.*

Focus on enjoying (and, umm, getting along with) your family at the dinner table. Always make room for dessert. Eff jello. I recommend Nutella--which I think should be a world currency. My friend, Rossella Rago, Host of the *Cooking with Nonna* show, http://www.cookingwithnonna.com/about/about-rossella-rago.html, would agree. She says Nutella cures all. Here is her recipe for her amazing Nutella-inspired cure.

Nutella Bouchee - Brownies

Ingredients:

- 1 Cup Nutella
- 2 Eggs
- 10 Tbs of all purpose flour
- 3 Tbs naturally sweetened cocoa powder
- Chopped hazelnuts or sliced almonds

Directions:

Heat your oven to 350 degrees and prepare a mini muffin pan with liners

In a medium bowl mix Nutella and eggs until well combined and smooth

Add in the flour and Cocoa and mix until smooth

Spoon the batter into liners and sprinkle with chopped nuts

Bake at 350 degrees for 10-15 minutes or until an inserted toothpick comes out clean

Step 6:

La Dolce Vita: Live The Good Life

Every breakup provides you with the opportunity to make a positive change in your life. You can transform your loss and pain into something beautiful and powerful. In essence, that is what I did with the creation of this book. Instead of throwing myself a perma-pity party, I decided to be the strong Italian American woman that I am. I decided that I would move forward and not only change my life, but I would inspire the transformation of others who struggled with heartbreak. I'd also have fun and be fabulous while doing it.

Those who know me know that I'm acting true to my character in sharing my experience and wisdom with others. Let's just say that if I'm having a party, I'm inviting everyone; it is going to be epic. Like many Italian Americans, I'm a social butterfly and usually say the-more-the-merrier. In my world, almost all strangers start out with the potential to be a business partner, referral source, lover, or paesano. (Note: *Potential.*) I love life and am passionate about living it to the fullest while sharing great experiences with others. La dolce vita, which translates to "the sweet life" in Italian, is what my paesanos and I strive to live 24/7. You should join us all, because living passionately is so much fun! There's no better time to make your life sweeter than after a breakup.

Living la dolce vita typically involves being surrounded by beauty, wonderful experiences, and the finer things in life. No one can deny the irresistible charm that is Italian. From the way food is savored during lavish meals to the way the fashions are worn, we Italian Americans have incredible passion and spirit! It is even reflected in the way we get around in our daily lives. No, I am not talking about the scooters and Vespas that the real Italians ride around in, but the Italian made performance sports cars that we all know and love in the U.S. including the Ferrari, the Lamborghini, and the Mazaretti. A*nd aren't those Fiat commercials so incredibly sexy?*

When Italian Americans travel around the globe, they travel in style. The luxury that is la dolce vita is apparent when you think of all the fabulous Italian fashion designers. Gucci. Prada. Cavalli. Dolce & Gabbana. Versace. Armani. Fermaggio. *Need I say more?* The sweet life may include all sorts of sensual pleasures, elegant home furnishings, and vacations around the globe. Even Jacuzzis are an Italian American invention!

Before you get your panties all up in a bunch, please note that the sweet life doesn't have to break the bank. Italian Americans have a talent for living well regardless of their geographic location or amount of money in their pocket. Sure, expensive perfume may smell better, but any fragrance has the potential to give you a pick-me-up. Surrounding yourself with beautiful things can come at any price tag. *And by all means if you can get yourself a discount, go for it.*

Before you learn how to live la dolce vita, you must realize that it is about far more than just acquiring material things and partying-- though there is nothing wrong with designer threads, the latest gadgets, or having a soiree on a gorgeous yacht! It isn't just about the glitz, glam, and labels though. The real problems occur only when people think material things are the key to their happiness. The Italian Americans know better than this and always have. We are people who care about other people--not just things. We also care about having unique experiences, learning, and enjoying cultural activities.

If you broaden your horizons, you will totally speed up your heart's recovery. Read books and magazines. See movies. Attend charity events. Go to the Opera. Get political. Support the causes that are near and dear to you. Find your talent. Serve people with it. Start a new business. Throw dinner parties with really formal invitations, go dancing in themed-costumes, have Bellinis at 11a.m. Kiss a stranger abroad. The possibilities for la dolce vita are endless! You can follow your passions and make yourself over into a different person--the one you always wanted to be. Pursuing interests that you abandoned when you were with your ex will be a real treat.

Living the good life can also mean throwing your heart and soul into your career, accomplishing big goals, and making your dreams come true. While there are many hobbies I would have loved to pursue post-breakup, my focus on my career became my saving grace.

When I was mending my broken heart, I took on more clients and added new services to my business including wingwoman sessions and mock dates. As a wingwoman, I go out with my clients to help them meet potential dates. Going anywhere from bars and lounges to museums or parks, I facilitate conversations for people looking to meet someone special. Not only is this a great time, but it is instantly rewarding as I get to see my clients succeed by getting phone numbers on the spot. With mock dates, I go on a simulated date with a client or hire someone else to do so. Afterward, I provide detailed and thorough feedback analyzing everything from the client's body language to dating etiquette to topics of conversation. (I really enjoy writing these reports, and my clients find this to be such a valuable and eye-opening service!)

In the meantime, I also continued to focus on getting new and interesting clients for the other services I was already offering--including image consulting, personal shopping, matchmaking, online dating ghostwriting, as well as dating and relationship coaching. Because what I do in my business is truly fun for me, it usually doesn't even feel like a job. Think about it: I get to work closely with my clients, pick out their clothes, select their dates, write flirty messages on Match.com, and laugh about dating mishaps or awkward first kisses the morning after. *Not a bad life!*

There is often an aspect of instant gratification to my work. There's the client who compliments me for making her sound a whole lot more interesting in her online dating profile than she really is. There's the ghostwritten message that gets a response in two minutes flat. There's the couple who thanks me for their first seven-hour date. This type of positive reinforcement just makes me strive for more.

Fortunately for me, the more I built my business; the more amazing opportunities came my way. There were several casting producers seeking me out for dating-related reality shows, radio and television hosts asking me to interview me, random bloggers contacting me with offers to guest post on my website, and plenty of other media opportunities. There were entrepreneurs I was starting joint ventures with. There were teleseminars I ran and articles I co-wrote. There were singles mixers I promoted and planned, dating seminars I co-hosted, and speed dating events I coached my clients through.

And, of course, there was an opportunity for me to experience one of my passions, traveling. Even better, this type of travel was the kind I could write off on my taxes! From accompanying a client to Saratoga to play wingwoman at the races, to meeting with dating coaches in Boston, to an all-expense paid trip to Chicago to appear on *WGN Morning News* and *The Mancow Muller Show,* I was experiencing it all. More and more, I was being treated like royalty as a result of my professional life. I was living it up in 5 star-luxury hotel accommodations, enjoying fancy dinners, and receiving expensive gifts from appreciative clients. *Guess who I was not missing?*

Without a doubt, a career you are passionate about is a surefire way to get over an ex. While this strategy works for all types of men and women, perhaps it is especially beneficial to women who have been socialized to rely on men to take care of them financially. Once a woman starts making her own *real* money, she becomes strong and independent enough to believe she can make it on her own. She empowers herself and becomes more selective about the men she lets into her life, because she knows she does not need a man to survive or be happy. *And just wait until she starts making "fuck-you money"....*

As Lady Gaga famously said:

"Some women choose to follow men, and some women choose to follow their dreams. If you're wondering which way to go, remember that your career will never wake up and tell you that it doesn't love you anymore."

Gosh, do I love Gaga!

While I believe it is love that makes us all happier than our career can in the long run, choosing to focus on career is a wonderful decision for many. Professional success leads to confidence. It leads to self-love, self-respect, and zero tolerance for bad behavior from others. With all of this in place, romantic love is likely to follow. Some say it is the other way around—that you find love and then find yourself. Sure, that can happen, but I think that type of love only lasts in the movies.

Another way to acquire self-love and live the good life is to have a religious or spiritual practice that gives your life a more meaningful existence. As for Italian Americans, we are, for the most part, Roman Catholics who believe that Jesus died on the Cross so we could be forgiven for our sins. Although generations past were very religious people, nowadays it seems that many define themselves as more spiritual than religious. Some just say peace, love, and compassion are their religion. Many Catholics are also known as "Cafeteria Catholics," because they pick and choose the parts of the religion that appeal to them.

For most, this means something along the lines of attending church on Christmas and Easter, skipping the sacrament of Reconciliation, following most of the ten commandments, and having sex before they are married. Many of these Catholics became disillusioned with the religion in their young adult years. They start to question everything and realize their beliefs conflict. Many choose football games over Sunday mass and feel they don't have to go to church to pray. There are many Italian Americans who get away from the religion for a while but become more religious when they or their family experience illness and tragedy. Many young parents get back to their religious roots, as they want their children to be baptized and practice as Catholics. Lately, there are many Catholics who have a renewed interest in attending church simply because they like the new Pope.

Despite the considerable number of Italian American Catholics who have lost their way, there are still many who are very serious about religion. These are the people who'd never think of eating meat on

Good Friday, who actually still give up something for Lent, and who make it their business to dip their hand in the Holy Water at the churches they visit around the world. They light candles for loved ones who are sick and say the rosary on the regular. They celebrate saints' birthdays. They save the palms from Palm Sunday. They wear crosses around their neck, make the Sign of the Cross, quote The Bible, name their kids after the disciples, and make all their sacraments. From Baptism and Penance, to Communion and Confirmation, to marrying in a church and getting the Last Rites, it is all a huge part of the Italian American way.

If you are Catholic, you may find some of these practices and rituals comforting when you are going through difficult times. You don't have to read as many prayer books as my mother does or say the rosary as often as my grandmother did, but it would not hurt for you to go to church once in a while. It might be good to kneel down and say Our Father, Hail Mary, or some variation of your favorite prayers. My own faves include:

"Now I lay me down to sleep, I pray for a man who is not a creep."

"Please God make him call or text."

"First, Lord, let there be no other women. Second, if there are other women, let them be uglier than me."

All lighthearted fun aside, my mother, as well as my Aunt Catherine, will be proud that I am suggesting you pray your way to brighter days! If you want to live la dolce vita, you've got to have faith that the relationship you had will not damage you forever and that you can find someone new to love. You can seek comfort in praying to God. *And not just when you want something.* Pray for strength, guidance, and protection. Pray for help in weak moments. Most importantly, pray to be spared the embarrassment of running into your ex.

If you aren't Catholic or religious at all, this talk of religion might be turning you off. Bear with me for a moment. I am not trying to act holier-than-thou or convert you into anything other than what you are. I just want you to know that you can borrow principles of Catholicism to help you move past your heartbreak even if you have a different faith or don't like organized religion. A basic understanding of this religion that teaches followers to be more compassionate toward others could provide you with the key to living the sweet life. For example, take the Catholic principle of forgiveness. If you hold grudges or have hatred in your heart, your quality of life will suffer. As the cliché goes, the only one you are hurting when you won't forgive is yourself. You may feel hateful toward your ex for what he or she put you through, but you have to get past it. You will eventually have to learn how to forgive your ex for his or her shortcomings.

Of equal importance, you must realize that forgiving your ex doesn't mean you have to be together or even be in contact at all. Releasing negative people and relationships from your life is a beautiful thing. Just because you no longer have certain people in your life does not mean you don't wish them well or do not forgive them. Sometimes, letting people go can be the most loving and compassionate act of all.

If you are still with me, another philosophy that may help in your recovery can be summed up with the following: "Let go and Let God." To put it simply, when you try to control too much in your life, you get frustrated when you do not get what you want when you want it. When you try to force the manifestation of your own wants, you get disappointed and angered when things don't work out your way. As you've probably realized, it is tremendously stressful to always try and make everything happen as perfectly as you want it to. But if you learn to go with the flow and start to want what God wants-or, in other words, whatever is happening in your life- the anxiety and all the negative emotions vanish.

When you have an open mind and realize that things are happening in your love life because they are the plans of God, or "The Universe" if you don't believe in God, you'll come to a place of peace and acceptance. You are not stuck in a battle where you are trying to play

God and make everything happen miraculously. Your mind is at ease. You can trust that everything will work out, because it is in the hands of a higher power. You will be extra grateful for what you have in your life when it comes from God. It will feel good—like it all makes sense. Think about it. If the relationship you had with your ex has filled you with heartache and sorrow, do you think it is what God wanted? Catholics believe God wants you to be happy and live a good life. Maybe you should believe it too!

Furthermore, getting tight with God can show you what la dolce vita is all about, because it will reveal important lessons to you. For instance, your faith in God will show you that you don't have to put too much pressure on yourself. If you haven't developed that faith, take my word that mental and emotional suffering is not necessary. Don't let society or your family have you believe that you have to go through a lot of suffering to be successful or happy. You should look for the positive in your situation, but you don't have to figure it all out. Things may not get easier, but you will get stronger if you just let God bring you what he wants. Be like the Italian Americans who are humble enough *not* to follow in the footsteps of (some) of their controlling ancestors. They recognize a truth that you should too. To put it simply, you don't have control over anyone or anything and should just leave things to God. You can let go if you stop dwelling on the past and how things will turn out with your ex. You need to accept that in the moment, things are the way they are; you are meant to be without your ex. You can stop trying to control when you start being mindful and present to what is going on right in front of you. Being in the moment is what la dolce vita is all about.

Sometimes what is right in front of you are people who could use some help, but you have to help yourself before you can help them. As the Catholics preach, living a good life is all about giving and receiving. At a church, parishioners put gifts under the Christmas tree for the needy children. They donate to second collections, bring in soup cans to fight hunger, as well as attend fundraisers, beef steaks, and bake sales for good causes. They say " Peace be with you" to their neighbors and offer up prayers to anyone who needs them. At the heart of the religion are people who are giving and receiving.

If you'd like to get into the spirit of giving, the first thing you should do is take care of yourself. As a wise man once said: "The greatest gift you can ever give another person is your own happiness." Sustainable happiness can be difficult for many of us, as we are bogged down by everyday life decisions like what chores need to get done, what calls must be returned, and which events we should attend. We have to take care of ourselves first if we want to be of service of others. If you are haunted by demons of your relationships past or currently stuck on an unhealthy ex that sucks the life out of you, it is going to be even harder for you to be able to give back. If most of your days are chaotic, and most of your interpersonal communication is unsatisfying, you are missing out on la dolce vita.

If you are thinking you should start living a life that involves following your bliss every day, you are on the right track. If you're chasing temporary highs, you're not grasping the lesson. You might just benefit from reading The Gospel every now and then. *Okay, sorry, I am not trying to shove it down your throat the way a Nonna would force you to clean your plate. Just sayin*! Do whatever it takes to be a happy person so you can get to a place where you could be of service to others. The more you help people, the more you will help yourself in your quest for happiness.

But before you start thinking about what you can give to others in need, realize what you need to give to yourself. If you are like most people, one of the most powerful things you can do to help yourself become a happier person is to improve your image; because when you look great, you feel great, and you invite greatness into your life.

Do you need some convincing?

Well, as a Dating, Relationship, and Image Coach, I am in the business of perception management. Image is all about the mental conception people have of you. It's what they think when you enter the room and what they say about you when you leave. I am fully aware that both outer and inner beauty is paramount in the way others perceive us. Are you? Have you ever walked into a high end boutique or department store dressed to the nines to find the same sales associates who barely looked at you when you shopped in sweats now bending over backwards to accommodate you? Did you score free drinks at a trendy lounge because your smile was extra inviting---before the pomegranate martini marathon? Have you seen what a fresh hair cut or blow-out could do to your confidence level when you are next to that cute stranger on line at the grocery store? *Now, that's what I call outer beauty!*

If your outer beauty is coupled with inner beauty-or what I like to define as the manifestation of one's unique, talents, gifts, and health of the body, mind, and spirit- you'll really shine like a star! Many Italian American men and women are stars. Just look around--Italian Americans are some good looking people! There's plenty of inspiration to be found. If you want to use an image makeover as a strategy for living the sweet life consider the following tips. Of course, when it comes to exes, living a happy life and looking good while doing it is the best revenge.

Create a unique personal style that is true to who you are

Yes, this implies that you must first and foremost know yourself. Like William Shakespeare said: "To thine own self be true!" While fashion fades with the changing of the seasons, influx of new designers, and the trends in the media, style is personally yours forever. It's not about looking like everyone else. Sure, you can buy the "in" pieces with the best of the fashionistas, but you can't buy style. It's that innate talent of knowing how to work them into your wardrobe. Do you know how to mix, match, and throw something together in less than five minutes for a big night on the town? If so, you are on the right track. Again, to quote Lady Gaga--who is, by the way, another fierce Italian American: "You were born this way, baby!" If you weren't so blessed, you can learn to have style.

Keep it classy, biatches

Men and women with true class epitomize elegance and sophistication no matter what their body type or budget. Being classy is all about being sexy without trying too hard. The classy man is the one that has two buttons of his crisp white polo open instead of four that reveal a plethora of unruly chest hair! (And go easy on the gold chains, guys.)

For women, keeping it classy means having a thorough understanding of the differences between sexy and slutty. It means leaving a little to the imagination to appeal to men. In other words, if you are revealing jaw-dropping cleavage, don't opt for the mini skirt! Never wear dark smoky eyes with dramatic red lipstick unless you are on the cover of *Vogue*. And don't underestimate the power of red lips!

Make sure everything is flattering

There is a lot to consider when creating an image that stands out. Of course, women have more options with hair, makeup, clothing, and accessories, but men these days have a lot to choose from as well. The most important things to consider when purchasing garments, products, or image-related services are fit and color. You should also consider the quality of the material, longevity, price, and practicality. The way an outfit fits can make or break your image. It's all in the little details like hemlines and sleeve lengths, and if yours are not working, you should definitely get yourself to a tailor. In order to have a fabulous appearance, you must develop an understanding of which colors go together and which clash. With a little education as well as trial and error, you'll be able to match everything from skin and hair tones to eye shadow shades and shirt colors.

Groom with greatness

I'm sorry, but you aren't great at grooming if you think brushing your teeth every day and making sure there are no remnants of chicken marsala on your pants leg will cut it! You should, in fact, brush and floss your teeth at least twice daily. and consider getting them professionally whitened. There is nothing like a mouthful of sparkling pearly whites!

When I say groom with greatness, I mean totally taking care of your body, mind, and spirit. When it comes to the physical, be sure to care for your skin; moisturizer and sunscreen are musts. Do the best you can with you hair. Keep it freshly cut and colored. These things matter so much when catching someone's attention. The little details count here too--please have neatly manicured hands. (At minimum, make sure your nails are evenly filed and cuticle-free.) Grooming with greatness could never be complete if it did not include getting proper rest, exercise, and eating a healthy, balanced diet. Make sure you are mindful of your emotional health too. See a coach or therapist to ensure optimal personal and professional development. Engage in beauty treatments that best align with who you are that are good for your soul! And, don't skip on that beauty sleep!

Mind your manners

As my dear Grandma LuLu would say: "Mind your p's and q's". Being polite has a tremendously positive impact on how the people you meet and date (or wish you were dating) perceive you. When you are in public, are you always texting on your phone? If so, how do you expect someone to approach you? Do you talk too loud or too much in a group setting? Do you drink too much when you are around new people? Do you chew with your mouth open or cover yourself in ungodly amounts of cologne that leave those around you gasping for air? If so, you are surely offending someone. You may even miss out on the opportunity to form a connection with the stranger who could potentially help you live the sweet life.

Think carefully about what you say and how you say it

Just like in the court of law, anything you do or say can and will be used against you when you meet new people! Over sharing is the biggest crime committed by singles in the initial stages of friendship and dating. (Talking too much about themselves and their exes comes in as a close second.) Even before they come to me, many of my clients know that they shouldn't talk about negative topics like family drama, past relationships, or health issues, but they get into these conversations anyway. *For the love of God, what is wrong with you people!?* Men and women need to learn how to proceed with caution when entering these murky waters of first date conversation. Situations can be reframed, new patterns of communication can be established, and more satisfying interaction can occur. Start by asking yourself: Are your conversations creating opportunities or threats in your quest for the sweet life?

Catch'em with confidence

You can, and will, attract people who will help you live the sweet life if you just get your swag on! "Swag," or what *Wikipedia* defines as the ability "to walk, talk or behave displaying a sense of confidence," is synonymous to "It" factor. You either have it or you don't! It's that inner strength and acceptance of who you are--that unshakable confidence--that keeps men and women everywhere coming back for more! Italian Americans definitely have it! If you feel like you lost a piece of your confidence after your break up-or never had it to begin with-you must work on cultivating it, because it is sooooo attractive! Have you ever come across someone who you just weren't able to take your eyes off of? Maybe he or she wasn't even the most attractive in the room, but there was just something about him or her, right? You couldn't even put a finger on it, but you wanted to see and know more. The key to creating the winning image that will get you to the sweet life is to have that confidence!

In this moment-and each and every moment-you have a choice to live the sweet life or some half-assed version of it. Only you can decide what is important to you and live out your values every day. It is up to you to take care of yourself and attract the people and fabulous life experiences that will allow you to be happy and live a beautiful life. While everyone is different, what follows are some ideas to get you started on your path to la dolce vita.

Action Steps to Live La Dolce Vita

Take inventory of your image, and make improvements where you need to.

Your Hair: Is it styled well? Is the style current?

Your Clothes: Do they fit well? Do they express your personality? Do they flatter you? Are they appropriate for where you are going?

Your Shoes: Are they clean? Do they match your clothes?

Your Skin: Do you have healthy skin? If you have an acne problem, be sure to take care of it.

Your Facial Hair: Are you clean cut or too scruffy and in need of a trim?

Your Nails: Are your nails trimmed and clean?

Your Body: Are you in shape or need to lose some weight to be healthy?

Your Smell: Do you smell good or does your scent turn people off?

Your Teeth and Mouth: Do you have good oral hygiene? Brush? Floss? Use breath mints? Need to whiten your teeth?

Your Posture: Do you have posture that shows confidence, or do you slouch and have uninviting body language? Are you afraid to take up space?

Your Voice: Do you sound confident? Do you speak up with a well modulated voice?

Your Brain: Are you able to keep a conversation going? Have a sense of humor? Pick up on social cues?

Make over your bedroom and suitcase.

One thing that can help you feel better, believe it or not, is to clean, organize, and virtually makeover your home. A lot of Italian Americans are neat freaks. Think plastic coverings on couches and Italian American grandmothers who vacuum their living room carpets daily. But let's think outside the living room to the area where you spent some time with your ex--your bedroom.

Your bedroom is your sacred space where you relax, sleep, and have sexy time. The décor and overall setting should be conducive to such. A messy bedroom, for instance, is a reflection of its' owner; a cluttered space is a cluttered mind. Your mind is cluttered enough after a breakup. If you unclutter your space, a peaceful mind will follow. You'll be less anxious if your bedroom does not serve as a constant reminder of you your ex, so make it over. A bedroom that epitomizes calm and opulence is the bedroom of someone who lives the sweet life.

Here are twelve ways to give your bedroom a makeover:

1. Tea light candles
2. 650 thread count sheets
3. Silk throw pillows
4. Luxurious bedding
5. A vanity with perfume/cologne in nicely shaped bottles
6. Incense
7. Dim lights
8. Ivory walls
9. The color red
10. Mirrors
11. Flowers

12. A chandelier

Another way to live the good life is to get out of the bedroom and see the world. Traveling can expand your mind and enrich your life in so many ways. Even a short weekend holiday could attract all kinds of positive experiences including romance. If you are looking for the latter or just want to feel your best, leave no stone left unturned when living la dolce vita in your travels. The secret to looking fabulous on vacation is all in how you pack!

Take it from the girl who used to lug heavy suitcases for just one weekend away–and ultimately be forced to play damsel in distress at staircases– packing light is better. Come on, you know you too have plopped down your bags at the bottom of an intimidating staircase waiting for an ever so gracious gentleman to come rescue you--as if that was not part of the plan! Chivalry is not dead, but you can't always count on it.

Here are my top three packing tips:

Think quality and not quantity. With clothing and relationships, it's the quality that counts. One weekend equates one pair of jeans. You can dress them up or dress them down with the right shoes and accessories. If you are going to the shore, you really only need two pairs of shoes. (And, yes, I do recommend the Jersey Shore if you want to meet some Italian Americans--not to mention have some good pizza and zeppoles.) Ladies, make them heels or cute flats for going out and flip flops for the beach. Men can wear dress shoes and sneakers or flip flops to the beach. To avoid over packing, choose good pieces like shirts that can easily transition from day to night.

Pick a color scheme. It's so much easier to pack and choose clothing that can take you from day to night when you color coordinate everything. Neutral colors, browns, blacks, and whites are the jetsetter's best friend. Don't be afraid to add a splash of color—especially if you are hoping to catch the attention of a cute and equally fashionable single. Make like a peacock and incorporate some bright colors into your outfits. Chunky bracelets or bangles and pink or turquoise costume jewelry can still work like magic for the ladies.

Make your products work double time! Are you that person who has to check a bag at the airport solely because of your beauty products? I have news for you: It's so much better to fit it all in the airport approved zip lock bag! (With most airlines charging to check bags, your wallet will thank you!) Whatever doesn't fit in your bag can be purchased at your destination. (Trust me; it will usually be cheaper.) In a pinch, body wash can also double as shampoo. (Don't listen to the stylists who say you can only use high end shampoos. Sometimes drugstore brands work just as well.) Reach for the moisturizer that also includes SPF, and buy the lipstick that can double as a blush. If you just get creative and switch up your beauty regime, you'll find the possibilities are endless.

Practice The Golden Rule: In order to live the sweet life, you have to treat people the way you want to be treated. In other words, "Do unto others as you would have others do unto you." [Matthew 7:12] Practicing The Golden Rule is the right thing to do, and not just for the sake of having good karma. (But let's be honest: What goes around comes around in relationships, so your motivation to avoid bad circumstances in the future might be strong.) When making a choice, you should consider the consequences of it. You should understand not only how it will affect you, but consider how it will affect others, if it will bring happiness, or if it will hurt them. Italian Americans, as family-oriented in nature as we are, often think about the greater whole. Let our loyalty and respect for our family inspire you to reflect the entire world of our brothers and sisters.

Step 7:

Attract a Better Match: How to Find Amore or Something Like It

By now, you know that your relationship ended because you and your ex aren't a fit at this time and most likely never will be. Since your ex is not for you, you'll eventually want to get yourself out there and find someone who *is* for you. There may come a point in which you'll realize you have to force yourself to go out to meet other singles. After all, there are few things as embarrassing as continuing to lust after someone who doesn't like you back. In time, you may get sick and tired of being embarrassed. Speaking of time, don't think that just because the idea of dating someone new hurts now that it will hurt forever. A love life that has not been all rainbows and butterflies doesn't equal a future that can't be totally amazing another time around. You can find a new love that is way better than the one before, and it can be totally be worth the pain. Love really is worth fighting for--unless it is with your stunad ex!

One day when you least expect it, you will be living la dolce vita and great love will happen to you. You won't believe how quickly your life will change or how you ever lived without this person you now care so deeply for. *That's amore!* When you meet that special person, you will truly understand why things never worked out with any of your exes. Until then, understand that there is a better match for you out there. In fact, there are a lot of potential partners you could be compatible with--even soul mates. You can look forward to finding your next relationship or even the love of your life sooner rather than later. But realize it probably isn't going to happen overnight.

It may take some considerable time to mend your broken heart to the point in which you could attract real love, though you are likely to attract some variations of it-from hookups to flings- in the meantime. Just getting over you ex could take months, could take a year, or could take half the length of your relationship or more. (A lot of people claim the latter.) Just as there is no magic number of days that will heal your heart, there's no telling when you'll attract a true match. As they say, you can't hurry love, but there are some things you can do to help it come along.

To begin with, if you want to find love, you need to know what type of person you want to be with and what kind of love you are looking for. While I am not here to force my ideas on you about the nature of the relationship that can make you happy or tell you exactly who you should be with, I must share what I know to be true about compatibility. I hope you can use my professional experience to your advantage. Since you made your way to the end of this book, let's assume you think I know something of value and should strongly consider taking my word. In case you are still on the fence, let me just share that in my nine years as a matchmaker and dating coach, I have seen and heard it all. I can tell you tons of different stories about people starting and ending love relationships. From the woman who stole a dish on her first date at a five star restaurant Manhattan, to the guy who got married three times and is still looking, to the couples who I've introduced that are living happily ever after, I have learned a lot from my involvement in peoples' stories. I've come to believe that a relationship generally has a higher chance of being healthy and happy for the long term when the couple is more alike than different.

I can see how opposites attract in some ways, but when it comes down to it, people who have similar core values, lifestyles, and visions for the future fare better for longer. The relationship will flow more smoothly when couples share some personality traits and interests, though it isn't necessary to have tons of things in common. Polarity is good for a relationship in some ways. For instance, dating someone in a different field can help you learn about a different industry and be less monotonous. However, people who are much more diverse than similar struggle to make their relationship work. If you want to attract your match, think of the things you value and enjoy most and find someone who is on the same page. If you are looking for an action step to help you figure out what to look for in a match, see my suggestions at the end of this chapter. Hint: You are going to make a wish list!

Since you are mending your broken heart Italian American style, you should look toward Italian American culture for clues as to what to focus on in the search for your match. Love, Italian American style, is one thing that is sure to help you get over your ex for good. As you may predict, I am of the opinion that Italian American men and women aren't too shabby in the dating and relationship department! We can make terrific partners, as there are a lot of awesome qualities we possess.

Whether you are hoping to date someone who is actually Italian American or resembles Italian Americans in some way, there is much to appreciate.

Let's start with the Italian American ladies. One reason men like them so much is because they love food and are excellent cooks. As mentioned previously, they like to make and enjoy great meals with family and friends. (Whoever said that the way to a man's heart is through his stomach was on to something!) Italian American women also appeal to men visually, as they are typically very beautiful, with olive skin, Mediterranean features, dark shiny hair, and slender frames. They make good friends, wives, and mothers, as they are caring and nurturing. Because they often come from big, loud families, they also know how to share, get along with others, handle conflict, and compromise when necessary. They also know how to put a man in his place. Even though some men may not admit it, most like a woman who won't have any of their bullshit. So keep your self-respect and sass, ladies.

As for Italian American guys, they can be so sexy and charming! It seems like women of all races and ethnicities are in cahoots about them, as they really know how to flirt and make a lady feel cherished. They aren't called Italian stallions for nothing! It is unanimous: The girls agree that the Italian American boys are really passionate in and out of the bedroom. It is fun to be with a guy who is confident and embraces life and the people around him. Also, women appreciate how Italian American men take care of them. As hard working and traditional men, they make great providers. Historically, if a lady wants to stay home and raise kids, her Italian American husband will step up and act as the breadwinner. Since many of the men have strong family values, as well as mothers who were housewives, they will do whatever they need to keep their family healthy, happy, and safe. They aren't afraid to throw themselves in their careers to make life easier for their wives and children. Sure, things have changed a bit since women started kicking butt in the workplace and some Italian American men may even be happy to play Mr. Mom. Yet the breed of Italian American male who would never let his girl pick up a check does still exist.

What's not to love about these qualities of an Italian American man or woman, right? Well, you don't have to date my peeps. You may date whoever you want. In fact, you can have a dating resume that resembles the United Nations for all I care. I just want you to date someone who deserves you that you have a shot at having a satisfying relationship with.

Let's break down the process a little more: Once you decide you are ready to attract your match and have identified the qualities you wish for, you have to make sure you (the product) would appeal to your target market before you put yourself in front of them. (If this attracting a match stuff sounds to you like it is all about marketing and public relationships, you are absolutely right!) If you want to date an Italian American, adopting some of the qualities of an Italian American man or woman will help your cause, because like attracts like; but you must go beyond that and find out what really speaks to the type you want to attract.

Before you focus on playing up the characteristics that would be a turn on to the type of man or woman you desire, you have to get rid of those that would turn them off. Any press is not good press when it comes to dating! There are certain traits that aren't just not good, but rather universally unappealing. A lonely, desperate, or needy vibe, for instance, is something most people dislike in a potential partner. To be an attractive single, you should realize that being single does not have to mean being lonely--even if you don't have many romantic options! Being single doesn't have to be forever, but if is for now, you should make the best of it. While you are on your own, you've got to focus a ton of effort on being as happy as you possibly can. Unhappiness is simply unattractive in the dating game.

FYI: Singles who go out on dates with a lot of people just because they are asked out tend to be unhappy. Don't fall into this trap. Know how to trust your gut and let it show you how to find love--first with yourself, then with someone else who actually meets your criteria. Putting yourself first and doing things that make you happy will make you more desirable. So if you would rather be at home washing your hair than having a conversation with a date who only meets three of your five match criteria, cancel your plans. If you'd rather not go out on a double date with your best friend and his girlfriend's co-worker, say so. The thing that you need a lot more than booking tons of dates you aren't excited about is hope! You have to believe in the power of staying true to yourself and what you are looking for. It is great to realize that timing is everything with dating, and that if you keep "doing you," you'll eventually meet someone perfect for you. This is the attitude to adopt if you want to stay positive and attract amore.

Just doing what will make you smile at this stage of life and putting a target market-worthy version of yourself out there ready to fight for love like an Italian American will give you a huge advantage. It won't be enough though, if you aren't in the right frame of mind for a relationship. The one thing that is perhaps the biggest turnoff to someone who is genuinely looking for love is dating someone who is not emotionally available. Therefore, doing the work to deal with your "stuff" and destroying anything that is blocking your ability to have true intimacy is essential to finding amore.

Exorcizing Your Ex

The biggest threat to your emotional availability is an attachment to your ex. A breakup provides a chance to learn from your past relationship, so that you can find a better fit and build your character. You have the opportunity to rebuild yourself even stronger than before, so that you are someone who can contribute to a great partnership in the near future. You can do this by analyzing your past relationship(s) and identifying patterns or trends. If this sounds a bit too deep and shrinky, you are in good company, as many Italian Americans would agree. Those would be the kind who are old school and don't believe in going to therapy, of course.

Being that I earned my master's degree in Marriage & Family Therapy and have let my clinical background impact the way I do my dating and relationship coaching and matchmaking, I clearly support the notion of therapy as an agent of positive change. When I was in grad school, I did nearly one thousand hours of clinical work counseling individuals, couples, and families. I never saw any of my therapy clients as weak for getting help, nor do I believe the clients who come to me now in a coaching capacity are weak because they seek out an expert to help them solve their problems. Rather, I think they are strong to let someone else into their lives so they could grow from adopting another perspective. Needless to say, if you choose to go to psychotherapy to become emotionally present and able to love, I support you one hundred percent. My sister, who also focused her studies and career in the mental health field, is another example of an Italian American who has a profound understanding of the benefits of psychotherapy. We are the Italian Americans of a newer generation who give therapy a thumbs up!

If you want to take a stab at channeling emotional availability using more of an old school Italian American approach, you do not need to go to therapy. I believe you can make great strides by doing it on your own with a little help from friends and family. The path to emotional availability starts with a commitment to seeking the truth about who you have been and who you want to be in your love life. You just have to be willing to go a little deeper to find the truth, as there is a deep reason why your relationship didn't work out. If you look within and around to heal yourself, the answers will be revealed to you.

The Truth, The Whole Truth, And Nothing But The Truth

If you want to grow, you have to embrace the truth—the whole truth and nothing but the truth. You need to know what didn't work for you in the last relationship, so you can visualize, in detail, a relationship that will work for you.

Your strategy for finding the truth is a choice you will make when you are ready to. There are really only two ways you can find out the truth: You can find out from your ex or you can find it out yourself.

Now, before I make suggestions for the recommended method of finding the truth, which is totally do-it-yourself, let me point out the obvious. You *can* contact your ex to learn more about the reality of your past relationship. Disclaimer: This is not advised--especially if it is soon after a breakup and you have not had sufficient time to properly work the steps. It is also really unnecessary, as you can't really learn anything from your ex that you don't have the ability to learn yourself. Anything that interaction with your ex reveals is something you already know deep down inside.

If you contact your ex, you can not do it with the hope of getting back together. In reality, getting in touch will not miraculously change anything. In fact, it will probably make things worse, so you really have to be prepared for the worst case scenarios. How would you feel if your ex totally ignored you? If your ex said something mean? If your ex rejected you again? What about if you saw that nothing changed and your ex just wanted drag you back into a circle that the two of you will run around in again and again? You have to be able to handle any consequence of contacting your ex, and you can't let it break you again.

Instead of taking this risk, strongly consider taking matters into your own hands. You can do this on your own. You have made it this far!

You can keep going. You can, once again, sit down and make a list to figure everything out.

My reasoning for these lists I am about to suggest you make: You need to see it in black and white to distinguish between the parts of your relationship that were reality and the parts that were fantasy. One list should describe who your ex really was in the relationship. You should remember your worst times including forgotten birthdays, belligerently drunk shenanigans, and the whole antipasto. Recall your ex's most irritating habits—the ones that made you cringe and contemplate a break up every time you experienced them. *Oh, and take a moment for gratitude while you are at it, because you'll never have to be annoyed by this nonsense again.* Another list should be about who you fantasized your ex was and another about the person you want to date in the future. You'll have a lot of comparing and contrasting to do if you really dissect your relationship.

If you don't sit down with a pen and paper, you run the risk of keeping everything jumbled up in your head. If you don't detangle and learn from your mistakes, you'll just make them again with someone else. A really helpful strategy in making sense of it all is to write down all the facts and events that took place since you met your ex. You should record all major interaction leading up to the breakup. If you have even an inkling that you may be leaving things out or misconstruing what really happened, you need to check yourself. If you've kept a journal throughout the relationship, you can go back and reread your past entries for clarity. If you were seeing a therapist or coach when you were with your ex, you can ask him or her to offer some perspective. If you don't have these luxuries, you can talk to your friends and family in order to validate the truth. Go through your list with your best friend, and see if your list matches up with his or her view. Post breakup, you have a lot of questions to answer, and it doesn't hurt to get several other opinions. Once you fill in your blanks and figure out what really happened with your past partner, you'll be more emotionally available for your future partner.

After you have overcome the weaknesses and threats to finding and keeping a healthy love, you are ready to focus on highlighting your strengths as you meet other singles. Show off the things that make you desirable to the man or woman you'd like to date. In order to do this, you have to know some more about what is desirable to virtually all men and women--Italian American or not. While men and women are diverse creatures with different needs, preferences, and backgrounds, there are some things that most members of each sex want in a partner. It is to your advantage to know those things, so read on….

Men are generally a little simpler in terms of their match criteria than women, though some are super picky. When it comes down to it, most don't ask for much. If you can understand how to appeal to the male psyche, it will be easy to figure out how to make them want you. Without a doubt, men fall in love with their eyes. Whether you think this is fair or not, if you are woman looking for love you need to exploit this universal truth and invest your time into looking as gorgeous as you possibly can. Fortunately, many men can appreciate all different types of beauty, and you don't need to be a size zero or eighteen year old supermodel to turn on a man visually. Most men like a woman who is naturally beautiful and confident in her own skin.

You don't have to wear a ton of makeup, but using some mascara, eyeliner, or lip color to play up your features is always a good thing. To be comfortable with your body, you should do your best to stay fit and toned. Accentuate your womanly curves. Wear stylish clothes that fit your shape and are well tailored. Pay attention to little details like hemlines and nail chips, and do whatever you need to do to fix them so you look well put together. Develop your own sense of style and rock it-- no matter where you are and what you are wearing. Be classy, feminine, and hint at sex appeal. Always look your best when you see a guy you are interested in.

However, if you want to attract a man for the long term, you need to be more than a pretty face, as looks are not the only reason why a man wants to be with a woman. If a woman has an unattractive personality, her shelf life will be short. Men want women who are lighthearted, fun, flirty, and positive. Women who are a pleasure to be around have the most appeal, as men want someone to laugh with, enjoy common interests with, and just kick back and relax with. Men don't want to be criticized, nor do they want to put up with moodiness and drama. They need to feel like men and don't want a woman to be too aggressive, competitive, or bossy. They also need to feel special and cared for. If you can look beautiful and figure out how to be easygoing, fun-loving, even-keeled, and supportive, you can figure out how to attract a man.

Likewise, a man can use good looks and personality to help make a woman want him, but there's got to be more than just what's at the surface to really capture a woman's attention for the long term. Generally women place less emphasis on a partner's looks than men do. They are more likely to have someone grow on them, as they can fall in love with personality and what they hear, as opposed to just what they see. Women tend to want guys who are extroverted-though not necessarily the life of the party-who are charming and have a presence. All types of women are attracted to alpha males who know how to take charge and lead them. They often want a man who is successful and powerful so that they can be taken care of and have a comfortable lifestyle. In general, they like a man for his smarts. If he can show her that he is socially intelligent, witty, thoughtful, and can make her laugh, he has a good shot at winning her affection.

To attract a woman romantically, it is crucial that a man makes a stellar first impression in dating, and his actions speak louder than his words. Love it or hate it, the woman is the one who gets to determine whether sex happens or not. Actually, allow me to rewind there: Rumor has it that women know somewhere between ten seconds and five minutes whether or not they'd sleep with a guy. Of course, this time frame is an estimate, but the point is that women size up men pretty quickly. They want to see a guy have manners and treat them well, but they also want to imagine that he'd be a passionate kisser who could rip their clothes off. Women instinctively know whether the man in front of them is destined for friend zone or something more romantic. A man may be able to change his fate if he is well-dressed and has the game of a Casanova. It is not just the clothes and charisma that make the man, though. But it is confidence, manners, intelligence, a sense of humor, graciousness, sex appeal, and generosity that all couple together to make a man irresistible.

In order to get the girl, guys also need to know the script that single women have in their head. In other words, they need to live up to their expectations of how a guy should act. If the guys are not doing things right-even little things like taking initiative to plan the date or coming to the girl's neighborhood to meet her, etc.-they are doing things WRONG. Men who don't follow the dating rules and norms generally aren't getting relationships, aren't getting second dates, and they certainly aren't getting any of *thaaaat. Sorry, but that's just the way it is--unless you are, of course, George Clooney.* If you want the Cliff Notes version of Dating 101 for men, it is this: If you are a guy hoping to win the affections of a special lady, treat her like one. Focus only on her and don't even so much as notice another woman when you are in her presence. Don't make a move too soon. Don't let her walk on the street side. Give her a twenty dollar bill for the cab ride home and your jacket if she is cold. Avoid discussing religion and politics on the first date. *And for God sakes, don't talk about your ex...*Better yet, stop talking and listen to what she has to say. Compliment her, and make her feel like the most beautiful woman in the room. Don't wait three days to call her. Show her how you feel right away. Never forget that a real woman only wants a man who wants her.

Meeting Other Singles

Now that you know what men and women want, do you know where to meet them so you can go show them you've got what it takes? If you are serious about finding love, I suggest you take a three- tiered approach which consists of meeting potential dates online, offline, and through matchmakers--whether they are friends, family, colleagues, or professionals love brokers.

To begin with, lots of modern-day technologies are available to singles looking to meet their match. Even if you'd prefer to meet someone the old-fashioned way, you can't deny that you probably have a better chance of meeting compatible partners by joining the forty million singles who've tried online dating than hoping to lock eyes with "The One" from across the room. Internet dating is very popular, because it is an efficient, low-cost way to screen potential relationship candidates. If you are looking to meet a large volume of people who are interested in dating, you can accomplish this by logging on to well-known sites like Match.com, Jdate.com, Plenty of Fish.com, Okcupid.com, or MillionaireMatch.com.

Keep in mind, success in dating is about quality and not quantity. Meeting large quantities of singles that lack the qualities you are looking for can sometimes make you feel lonelier--but not as lonely as you'd feel lying in bed next to someone who is all wrong for you. *Like your ex. Cough Cough.* When you are feeling lonely, you might be tempted to book yourself with dates every night of the week. This could be a great way to meet new people, but it could also cause you to fall victim to trying to change your single status by becoming a serial online dater. This type of compulsive dating tangles you up into a web of perpetual singleness. If you find yourself going on a ton of Tinder dates and to as many parties as possible-in fear that if you don't you may miss out on the love of your life- you are actually doing a disservice to yourself.

So stop with this common pitfall of single hood right now, as it will sabotage your chances of finding love. There is a paradox of choice at play, and meeting more and more singles won't necessarily help you find your soul mate.

To attract the right singles on an online dating or mobile dating site, make over your profile with my expert tips:

Get better photos. This is first and foremost, because everyone is a visual creature when deciding who to date on the internet. Your photos should be classy—not trashy! Ladies, don't reveal too much cleavage, wear too much makeup, or pose in unnatural, seductive photos--like those of the MySpace "kissy face" generation! Men, keep your shirts on and crop out the beer bottles and scantily-clad women next to you. Whether you decide to get professional headshots or have friend snap some of you on your digital camera, make sure you create a profile with a variety of recent, flattering photos that are true to who you are.

Choose the perfect profile length. Ladies, if your profile is too long, men will pass it by. Most men don't even like texts that exceed 160 characters. Write anything that resembles a chapter in your first novel and they will be on to the next. The idea is to intrigue them enough to make them want to know more—not share your life story. Men, if your profile is too short, you probably come across as boring and generic sounding. Also, you are no help to the woman who is a great catch, but has no clue what to write to you! A couple paragraphs with a little personalized detail goes a long way for both sexes, because when you include open-ended questions and interesting comments, you are giving him or her the perfect bait. Not too long, not to short—but just right.

Give yourself an attitude check. One thing a healthy and happy single looking for a great relationship doesn't want is to bring drama and negativity to his or her life. You may not think of yourself as the Drama King/Queen type, but the frustrations of the online dating scene can turn you into one. If you make statements in your profile like "I don't play games," men and women will think you do, in fact, play games. They will assume you have baggage and insecurity due to bad experiences in past relationships. *Otherwise, why would you write this?* Other than sounding negative and "crazy," you don't want to come across as high-maintenance or arrogant. Think light-hearted and fun—that way he or she will actually want to date you!

In addition to your efforts to try and attract your match online, you should also go out and meet people in the real world. The truth is, you can find love anywhere--at the gym, on the train, or in the grocery store, while waiting to pick up your morning coffee. Get into the warm and friendly Italian American mindset and scope out some strangers to make friends with. You have to put your antenna up and look for people who are receptive to meeting someone new. Unfortunately this can be hard, as more and more people are texting away on their Iphones or otherwise caught up in their own world, not wanting to be bothered in everyday places.

If you can find a friend that you enjoy spending time with, go out to meet new people together. It is bound to be a fun adventure. If he or she has also recently gone through a breakup, it will be even better. By the way, these people shouldn't be too hard to find. Let's face it: Unless all the couples you know are getting married, someone is getting dumped. That means there's someone out there you know personally-or through six degrees of separation-who would love to go mingle with you.

When I was in the midst of trying to mend my own broken heart, I forced myself to go out a lot. At one point, I committed to going out once weekly in NYC with a girlfriend who was also trying to live in an ex-free zone. We made the perfect man-meeting pair. She's platinum blonde. I'm jet black. She's a little older. I'm a little younger. She lives across the Hudson. I'm on the Upper East Side. We both wanted to meet some new men- sophisticated and successful professionals-so we would go to hotel bars and upscale steakhouses at happy hour to check out the scene.

After work, I'd trade my sensible black pumps for some fun stilettos I could barely walk in and meet her at the midtown venue of the week. She once brought me a pink Rose Quartz stone, which is known to bring self love and romantic love into one's life--even more so when received as a gift. I once brought her a bottle of perfume that I used to wear at a time in my life where I was at the height of my man-magnetism. (Call me superstitious. I think these details matter.) Mostly, we would bring ourselves, our wingwoman skills, and our game faces. We'd exchange bad date stories, diss our exes, and share ridiculous text conversations while waiting for men to approach us. We'd meet married guys who weren't wearing wedding rings, generous Manhattan finance guys who'd cover our $20 cocktails on their company black cards, and down-to- earth Jersey boys who'd shell out the cash for the round of shots they hoped would make us like them. Even though it was rare that we'd meet someone dateable, we'd always have fun and good stories for our friends. The day after one of our outings, my inbox would include a message like this:

"Did you ever hear from the drunk older man the other night who said you remind him of his dead wife?"

Just for the record, no, I did not. However, *we* did hear from the drunk younger guy who texted us *both* "Sup?" at 12:30AM, hours after we met him. (In case you are wondering, we did what any respectable lady would do—fail to respond.) *Oh, the singles scene in NYC!* You've got to love it! If you would like to try going out on some Girls or Boys nights in Manhattan to meet some fresh faces and have great dates that will help you forget all about your ex, let me let you in on a not-so-secret-secret or two.

When I first began my career as a NYC matchmaker back in 2005, I quickly learned how difficult it is to from romantic relationships in NYC. I found that most singles work super long days-even on weekends-just to pay their rent, live their lifestyle, and gain the competitive edge in their industry. Although they are uber-focused on work, they make time to play too—with multiple partners! Despite all of their dating options, New Yorkers have a hard time forming successful, long term relationships. They go on one online date on Monday, another on Tuesday, another on Wednesday; don't even get me started on their weekend activities! The combination of the Internet and being out and about in the big city meeting singles naturally at events and parties has them overwhelmed to the point in which they don't take any one option too seriously. It is not rare when seemingly great first dates don't lead to seconds--for no good reason at all. It's a single's scene where first dates are a dime a dozen, and one small bump in the road equates a deal breaker. People are quick to say goodbye, because there is always someone else waiting around the corner. The competition, especially among women looking for relationships, is fierce.

Indeed, attempting to meet singles through NYC nightlife venues requires a single to have thick skin, and not just because of the rejection that comes from people at clubs who are seldom looking for relationships! Allow me to explain: If you've ever been out in the city's meatpacking district, you know there are places that are very difficult to get into unless you are friends with some well-connected promoters. For instance, have you ever tried to get into a trendy club without being in a group of gorgeous, half-naked, modelesque women or the desire to drop 5K plus for a bottle of Grey Goose? *Yeah, good luck with that! By the way, is anyone else sick of all those vodka-crans, or is that just me?* Chances are, if you try to get into a venue without any of the above, you'll be turned away at the door. Don't sweat it though. You can't really take it personally when you are dealing with some silly guy who got beat up in high school and turned into a bouncer on an ego trip.

If you're single and hoping to change that status, I am pretty sure you should think beyond clubbing and attend an actual singles event at least once in your lifetime. Not only will you be in a place where everyone attending is actually single-and will therefore increase your chances of scoring a match-but you will likely get a boost in self-esteem. On one hand, you'll acquire some confidence from the compliments you're likely to get; on the other, you'll have your swag on in full effect just because you are surviving and thriving in such an environment. As in when living in NYC, if you can make it here, you can make it anywhere. You'll have a much better chance of surviving and thriving if you obey my six codes to live by when attending singles events.

I wholeheartedly suggest you put the rules that follow in place, because they WORK! They've worked for me, they've worked for my clients, they've worked for my friends, and they can work for you!

Here they are:

1. *Dress to impress!* Your look is paramount when attending a singles event. There are a bunch of singles competing for a limited pool of men or women; may the best dressed win! You don't need to be a full-out

fashionista or dress only in the hottest brands, but you do have to create a polished image and stand out from the crowd.

2. *The party don't start 'til you walk in.* Plan to arrive at the event on time, but don't stress if you end up getting there a few minutes later than you planned. You bring the fun. Walk in like you mean it; watch where your grand entrance will get you. And remember: It is better to be late than arrive ugly.

3. *Check your negativity at the door.* Erase any negative thought from your brain and replace any negative word in your vocabulary. It doesn't matter what went wrong earlier that day, you are there to make a positive impact on your love life. No one wants to hear your sob story. So smile, and be happy! If you play your cards right, you may get some sexin soon! Ha! *Seriously, though!*

4. *Everyone has value.* Any person you meet is a potential friend, business partner, client, messenger from God/The Universe, cupid, or love of your life. Don't frown because the guy or girl you have your eye on is interested in someone else, because you'll miss out on the greatness of the person right in front of you.

5. *Don't wear out your welcome.* Just because you are at a singles event does not mean that every single person there wants to talk to you for extended periods of time. It is not a "meat market" with a free pass to approach anyone you want and monopolize his or her time. Most are there to meet several prospects, so learn how to start and end conversations in a timely fashion. If the person you are talking to looks bored (i.e. eyes roaming around the room as you speak) politely thank them for the conversation and move on to the next. If you are the bored one, don't feel bad about cutting a conversation short.

6. *If the venue sucks, just leave.* If your goal is to meet people and no one is there but one couple who needs to get a room and one unattractive old man who is looking at you like he recognizes you from SeekingArrangements.com, just make a graceful exit, pronto. If you feel bad about walking into a bar, not ordering anything and leaving, offer

the bartender a polite smile. Ask when is a better time to come back; then make a run for it.

7. *Stay sober.* A smart single does not get drunk at a singles event. Keep a two drink maximum if you have a tendency to get sloppy. Drink water in between drinks. Get your Italian American on and have a meal before the event or munch on snacks there. If getting a little buzzed will help you loosen up and be more social, so be it. But remember, there is a fine line. You can get elegantly wasted once you are in a relationship, but until you get there, go easy on the booze.

Lastly, you can attract your match by relying on matchmakers to make the introduction for you. Humans are better at making quality introductions than a computer, if they understand what the people they are introducing are looking for. You can get great matches from your friends, family, and colleagues, if they have social circles that include the type you'd like to meet. This matchmaking will only work for you if people know you, your potential match, and both of your matchmaking criteria inside and out. Because many people just match their friends with others who are single and of their religion, age range, or geographic proximity, people turn to professional matchmakers to get more personalized introductions. Of course, there are many benefits to working with a matchmaking service, as they have larger databases than any of your friends and are trained to screen efficiently as well as use their intuition and experience to find you someone compatible. Keep in mind, whether the matchmakers you enlist are amateur or professional, it is crucial that they truly understand the kind of relationship you want.

Telling a potential matchmaker that you want an amazing relationship that will last a lifetime with a kind-hearted person isn't going to get you anywhere. You need to be specific. If you are looking for someone who can be half of a power couple, who will work on business projects with you, live with you in multiple locations, travel around the globe, and start the next great non profit, say it. (*By the way, if you know this guy, send him my number. Seriously.*) If you want someone balanced who takes excellent care of his or health, there is nothing wrong with asking for someone who loves the gym. If you want to have children or feel like teenagers in love when you are with your partner, tell your matchmaker that too. The point is if you want to succeed, you must have open and honest communication about your preferences, needs, and deal breakers with anyone matching you up. You have to know exactly what you want to get it.

Remember, if you don't stand for something, you fall for anything. Italian Americans don't fall for bull shit, and you shouldn't either. If you want to find love, you can't waste your time dating people who you'll never share it with. Finding potential matches is just the first step to finding true love. As you are dating, you have to read signals, interpret behavior, and determine if the person you've been seeing is worth pursuing a relationship with. You'll have to decide whether giving chemistry a chance to develop with someone you are dating is preferable to dismissing a potentially good/man or woman who you don't feel instant fireworks with. You'll have to decide if red flags should end the game or just be a warning to proceed with caution. You'll have to know when you should call back and when you shouldn't call at all. Dating for the purposes of finding amore isn't easy, so it is important to manage your expectations. A lot of "stuff" will come up for you when you are dating post-breakup. You'll be seeking closure on the past and answers for the future at the same time.

Without a doubt, when in the process of getting over an ex and trying to attract a match, there will be times when you feel a super strong need for answers. You'll want to know if the person you are seeing is for you or if your ex is thinking about you, if your ex is dating someone else, if your ex's relationship will last, and if seeing your ex would bring closure or open the door to getting back together. You may start to feel anxious not only when thinking about your ex but when thinking about certain scenarios with the new people you are dating. If you start dating someone new before you are ready to, you may experience anxiety around how the relationship is developing. You may wonder if he'll call, when she'll want to hook up, if the whole interaction will just result in another heartbreak and so on. If you just experienced your first heartbreak, all of these feelings will be strange and new. They are really quite normal, though unhealthy and likely to lead to self-sabotage. (Not to mention the failure to launch a new relationship!) The first cut really is the deepest.

If you are desperately seeking answers, you may be tempted to do something the older Italian American family members may disapprove of. No, I am not talking about interracial dating! *Ha.* I am talking about calling a psychic. Psychics happen to the best of us, but the best things don't always happen when we contact them. (If you want evidence, just go to RipOff Report.com and look up California Psychics!) Don't get me wrong, I do believe some people have God-given psychic gifts and use them to help others in tremendous ways. However, there are lots of scam artists out there who just tell people what they want to hear. Thanks to the Internet, you can do your homework to make sure you aren't getting ripped off by some gypsy who wants you to buy crystals that will help reunite you with your lost love. Yes, I've had more than a psychic reading or two; but when they started talking about jealous friends who put a spell on me, I was so out of there!

If you want to get over your ex Italian American Style, you aren't going to be calling any psychic hotlines. As my mother reminds me, consulting with psychics seems to go against the Catholic religion. As many old school Italians would explain, psychics aren't God and therefore can't predict the future. If you want to honor the culture of the motherland, the last thing you are going to do is waste $8.50 per minute pouring your heart out to someone in the UK named Destiny. Instead, your destiny will be soon revealed if you leave it in God's hands. If you feel tempted to call a psychic, try calling a friend or making friends with a therapist or relationship coach. If your friends don't answer, don't despair. You can always call on the man upstairs. Let's face it, the nights can be lonely when you are in your bed all alone and yet another potential match has disappointed you. Feelings of sadness can creep up on you when everything slows down. Before you start wallowing in self-pity, quiet your mind. Don't try to make any decisions in your current state of mind. Just say a prayer and sleep on it. You might just wake up with the answer you've been waiting for that will lead you to your true love.

If you are still waiting for your prayers to be answered-or aren't as much of the praying type as my Italian American bestie who says she will pray for me every time I meet potential husband material-let me clue you in. You don't really need any psychics to find out who you should be with, because when someone wants to be in your life, they put themselves in it and stay there!

Let me paint another picture that may look nothing like your past relationship: If someone likes you, they care about impressing you. For instance, in the early stages of dating, a man who likes a woman might go the extra mile in planning dates. He may take her to the hottest restaurant in town or plan a picnic at the park. He'll look his best and get his hair cut, and so will she. Whenever they get together, they will make sure it is special. As the relationship progresses, a couple that is really into each other will put in effort to get to know each other's friends and family. Ideally, a man will plan weekend getaways and buy his girlfriend thoughtful gifts for no reason at all. He'll always go out of his way to give her the best of everything that he can, and she will do the same. She'll come up with all sorts of sweet little gestures to make his life better, and he'll never give up on being generous with his time, money, and effort. She will make him want to be a better man, and he will make her want to be a better woman. If a guy really cares for a woman, he'll try to make her life better, and she will regularly do the same for him. It will come naturally for them both. It is his nature as a male to want to solve problems for her, and as a female she has a nurturing instinct that will lead her to do all sorts of sweet things for him.

While no man or woman is perfect, and all relationships don't subscribe to such relationship (and gender-based) ideals, a true love relationship will bear some resemblance to this picture. If you aren't experiencing something similar, you have to ask yourself if the person you are dating is showing he or she really cares about you.

When two people really care about each other, everyone knows about it. The couple will make it clear that they think about the big picture. They will do things to support each other's dreams. They will put up with each other's foul moods and forgive each other when they do wrong. They'll sacrifice their own needs and desires to make each other happy.

If your relationship looks nothing like this, you've got to consider whether the relationship could really go the distance in the good and bad times. If you have to ask yourself if this relationship is *it*, it probably *isn't*.

After all, if it doesn't feel right, it is wrong. One this is clear: At this point, you should be close to the place in which nothing should feel more wrong than being with your ex.

Action Steps You Should Take To Attract Amore Or Something Like It

Make a Wish List.

During the Christmas season, children make lists for Santa Claus. There is definitely a magic to this list making, as it helps the children attract what they wish for. They don't always get everything they want, but many get the majority of toys on the list.

It wouldn't hurt for you to make a wish list of your own, and you don't even have to wait until the holidays! While it is good to be mature, realistic, and transcend the superficial when making your list, embrace your inner child and ask for whatever you want. Don't judge yourself. You can't help some of the characteristics that impress you.

Want some inspiration? I'll share: My wish is to marry a TDH (tall, dark, handsome) alpha male, who is smart, witty, romantic, fun, can make me laugh until my stomach hurts, be a great provider, share my penchant for la dolce vita, and never fall out of love with me. Bonus: Italian American. Note: I do deviate from this type in my quest to find real love, because sometimes you never know who you may hit it off with! *And at the end of the day, hair color doesn't really matter now, does it?* Besides, there are plenty of other practical things that really, really matter to me in my search for Mr. Right.

If you are a single marriage-minded lady, they should probably matter to you too!

Drum Roll please…………

My Wish List includes a man:

With Integrity: My belief is that a man is only as good as his word. If he lies to me once, he could lie to me again. I think a woman should not tolerate any sign of disrespect from her man.

Who Is Loyal: I shared my toys since I was a little girl, but a man is not a plaything. I refuse to share my man with another woman. Infidelity is my deal breaker of deal breakers. And that "Once a cheater always a cheater" thing? Well, there are some exceptions, but it is not exactly a myth either!

Who Wants The Real Deal: I want a healthy, happy, lifetime partnership that is complete with friendship, true love, marriage, and kiddies. (Okay, ideally, I want children, but finding true love with the right partner is more important to me than just being a mom for the sake of experiencing motherhood.) I don't want the man who just wants the challenge. How about you? If he's just in it for the thrill of the chase, do you really think you are winning?

Who Is Emotionally Mature: Attention to all potential male suitors; I do not work for free! While I used to have a penchant for diamonds in the rough, I am a changed woman who will no longer accept a man with the potential for emotional maturity. If I'm no longer willing to teach a guy I date how to treat a woman and I'm *a dating coach*; why should you be?

Is Generous: Generosity, according to me, must be across the board. I want a man who is generous with his time, money, and affection.

Scrooges need not apply. You should only make a man as important to you as you are to him. If he isn't generous, he shouldn't be important. Period.

Is Supportive: Ya know those narcissistic guys who want everything to be about them, them, and them? *Check, please!* I can spot them from a mile away and you should too. If he doesn't show that he cares about you, your interests, your work, your hobbies, and your needs on the first few dates, dating him will not be a picnic. Run now!

Has A Good Head On His Shoulders: There are many types of intelligence. One that I really value in a man is common sense. His life needn't be perfect, but there are some things he just can't be. My deal breakers include an addict in denial, a man who is irresponsible with finances, a guy who is reckless with people's emotions, or just plain dumb in everyday situations. Don't you want a man with common sense so you can respect him as well as feel protected?

So there's my wish list, now get to yours!

Let your old relationship rest in peace.

R.I.P., or "rest in peace" is often found on the graves of Catholics. The idea behind this expression is to offer rest and peace to someone who has died. Likewise, a relationship can rest in peace if you just leave it alone. Letting go is often easier when you have the answers to some tough questions. Ask yourself the following so that you can learn from your relationship and put it to rest:

What were the problems in the relationship with your ex?

What problems did your ex have with you?

What did you dislike most about your ex and how he/she treated you?

What did you put up with that you shouldn't have?

What were you blind to about your ex that you now see?

Why did the relationship fail?

What still hurts?

What is your role in what hurts?

What choices did you make to get there?

What did you put up with that you shouldn't have?

How did you teach your ex how to treat you?

What changes do you need to make to get over your past relationship?

How do you need to heal?

What part of the relationship do you want to leave in the past forever?

What do you need to do to get closure?

How can you both be better now that you are apart?

What would you like to do different in your next relationship?

What traits about your ex do you miss and want in your next relationship?

Remember: Put yourself out there in a place where you can meet other singles. Just do it.

Getting In The Last Word:

Badda Bing, Badda Boom

Heartbreak happens. Your experience with your past relationship is either going to hold you back or move you forward. By now, I hope my depiction of strong, proud, passionate, hard-working Italian Americans has inspired you to put in a good fight for the cause of getting over your ex.

Adopting the Italian American style of mending a broken heart is just what you need, my paesano, and this book gave you all the tools you need to succeed. But be warned: Even when you make considerable effort to move on by following all seven steps as best as you can, exes and the people and things associated with them have a funny way of coming back to you.

Just when you think you are finally rid of them, they reappear in your life—to repeat like that garlic sauce you had at Sunday Dinner. They get under your skin, make you question your sanity, and take you right back to that uncomfortably-comfortable place. Since you've made it this far and are pretty much Italian American in spirit, you would probably love to do what nearly all Italian Americans love to do: Get in the last word. The problem with doing this is that the last word is never just a last word with an ex you haven't quite gotten over. Instead of getting the closure you tricked yourself into thinking you'd get, your talks or meetings with your ex may open up a whole new can of tomatoes. Instead of your ex being someone else's problem, he or she remains your problem.

Listen up, Sweat Pea. The idea of your ex moving on will most likely pain you. After all, it can be extremely difficult to be happy about your ex being happy with someone else—especially if you haven't yet found your match. On the other hand, it can also be difficult when your ex is in a relationship with somebody else but isn't so happy. Especially if that means your ex is still thinking about you. And calling you. And texting you. And asking to see you. This is exactly what you want to avoid!

Of course you are uber-memorable, and I don't blame that stunad ex of yours for still wanting you in his or her life. I don't blame you if you enjoy the attention and the fact that you are "winning" because your ex is still thinking about you. Of course, if you aren't thinking about your ex as much as your ex is thinking about you, well, then you are *really* winning.

Sometimes when your ex is in a new relationship but is still trying to keep you in his or her life, the inevitable happens. His or her partner finds out. *Did I say finds out? I should have said flips out!* Of course this all leads to an awkward phone call, an impulsive email, or an uninvited knock at your door from the person who is now sleeping with your ex. Clearly, this situation will present some challenges. The way you handle it will be a testament to your growth or lack thereof. The best way to handle such a mess may be hard to determine at first. The solutions I propose may seem counterintuitive to your natural instinct. *Beat 'em up. Tell 'em off. Flip some tables, will you?* As previously mentioned, despite the urge to do so, you should never resort to violence. In fact, you should take the alternate route—also known as the high road. Taking the high road Italian American Style consists of two main practices:

Playing nice: Adopt the warm and friendly Italian American personality and make nice with this person your ex is currently dating. You don't need to have an enemy. If you met in other circumstances, maybe you'd even be friends. There is no need to become besties, but you can treat each other with common courtesy and respect. Remember that this person is going through a lot of drama dealing with your ex. You've been there, done that. If you don't want to go back to your ex and just want this conflict to stop, you should do everything in your power to deescalate the situation.

Your ex's partner is probably contacting you for one of two reasons: 1. He or she wants to know if your ex cheated. 2. He or she wants you to stop talking to your ex. Your ex is making his or her current partner feel insecure, and this person is doing everything they can to hold on to the relationship. It is either that or the partner is looking for evidence to leave the relationship. You do not have to be overly generous with your communication. If your ex's partner is rude to you, you don't have to take it. But you don't have to give it right back to him or her either. (You *so* have the last laugh here.) If the truth is that things are dead and gone between you and your ex (or at least for one of you), don't deny that.

Let it be known that you have moved on, or are at least trying to. Your ex's partner really just wants to know that you aren't trying to break up a happy(ish) home. So if you're not that kind of girl or guy, say it with conviction. You don't *really* want your ex back. So admit it. Say that you have better things (and people) to do! All you have to do is say it once and make it clear. Beyond that, it is outside of your duties in the job known as being a decent human being. You don't have to provide any further assistance. So just keep it simple. Let the truth be told—and told with a smile!

Stai Zitto or Keep Your Mouth Shut: Perhaps you are going to be talking with your ex's significant other, but you don't need to cackle on like a caccione. There are some things better left unsaid. Is it really necessary to reveal that your birthday wasn't the only day your ex reached out? If you are truly over you ex, there is no need to share the details that would only make things worse. Sure your ex has hurt you, but hurting your ex is not the type of revenge that will make you feel better. (But remember, living a fabulous life without your ex is.) If you aren't going to be with your ex, your ex might as well be with someone else. *Who cares who it is?* It will do you no good to sabotage his or her chances of relational bliss. A tell-all could be tempting, but that isn't the type of revenge that will make you happy. *And unless you are a Kardashian, who is going to read it?*

As the Italian Americans of the mobster variety would say: No one likes a rat! Taking the high road means not choosing action that will pain your ex. It means honoring the positive memories--no matter how few are left--that you still have of your ex. It means respecting your ex's right to happiness by biting your lip. It means not taking a hammer and beating to death every last iota of love you and your ex have for each other. (While we are on the subject of love, if it is true love you had for your ex, it is not going to ever completely go away. Through it all, you may always have that warm and fuzzy place in your heart for your ex. Just leave your ex there in your heart—not in your life.) When an ex's partner gets in touch, remember that the question of how much or how little to disclose will inevitably come up. The answer is real simple: Your loyalty is, in fact, to your ex and not the new bitch on the block. Don't make everything even worse by forgetting that. Just don't get it twisted: When it comes to exes, loyalty doesn't mean having to be together. It just means keeping your trap closed.

With all this drama, you may have to go backward to move forward in your search for the meaning of it all, but I could just spare you the drama by revealing that there is a reason your ex came back. It is usually not to haunt you forever or because you belong together. Quite the contrary, it is a lesson to be learned that will help you get more comfortable with being apart.

Until you've really put in a good fight for freedom of the ex, the spell your ex has on you will still live on. If you are tempted not to follow the steps in this book, say the hell with it, and just get back with your ex, **don't do it!** Now, more than ever, you have to recall the true nature of your stunad ex. Remind yourself that your ex was condescending, cheap, lazy, and didn't appreciate you, or that your ex cheated, lied, disappeared, and started dating someone else.

If your ex was physically, mentally, sexually, or emotionally abusive, you may have blocked some things out, but it is important not to forgettaboutit. Get your ass out of denial! NOW. If you find yourself fantasizing about the possibility of happily ever after, you have to remind yourself that your damaged relationship will not miraculously work itself out. You have to tell yourself that your ex is not *really* who you want, and that there is someone better out there for you. Even if you read this whole book and never bought into the whole-my-ex--is-a-stunad-thing, swallow this harsh truth: The person who dumped you-or forced you to dump him or her due to intolerable behavior- isn't The One.

Despite all of the negativity of your past relationship, I know a part of you may still hold on to some of the positive aspects with a tenacious grip. While you can intellectually move on from the idea of being with your ex as much as you want, your heart won't move on until your heart wants to move on. You can know with certainty that going back with your ex in any capacity will set you back emotionally. You can predict that you will feel unloved after the love drug wears off. You can imagine feeling shame over your friends and family potentially finding out what you are considering, you can experience guilt and anxiety over the idea of having sex with your ex, and embarrassment for acting foolish and swallowing your pride. You can do all these things….. and still go back to your ex.

On the other hand, you can choose to rewrite your story--just like I rewrote mine. *Again and again.* You, too, can realize the beauty in the breakups with each and every one of your exes.

According to the American poet, author, screenwriter, and playwright, Carol Pearson:

"Most of us are slaves of the stories we unconsciously tell ourselves about our lives. Freedom begins the moment we become conscious of the plot line we are living and, with this insight, recognize that we can step into another story altogether."

You are now conscious of your plot line. You have a choice to make. You can decide to move forward by choosing not to look in the rearview mirror. Or you can continue to look back and waste days, weeks, and months on your ex. If you know you are well on your way to getting over your ex and don't want to get in touch and risk the possibility of your ex thinking you are still in love with him or her, that is a good sign you are going onward and upward. If you don't want to give your ex the satisfaction of knowing he or she even crosses your mind, even better!

As you go through the healing process, there will be ups and downs. There will be setbacks that make you sick to your stomach, but they won't hurt you as much as the pain of getting back with your ex. There will be moments of victory, but winning will never taste as sweet as the moment you realize you are done with all of the pain.

To get to la dolce vita and find long-lasting amore with someone new, you have to get to the point where you've just had enough of putting energy into anything having to do with your ex. You have to be done with the person you used to be. The most empowering thing to remember is that if you want the suffering to be over, it *will* be over sooner rather than later. You've got to really be hungry for it though. You've got to fight with all you've got. You can't give up just because healing may take longer than you ever imagined. You can't stop believing in the power of freedom of your ex. You must realize that the struggle is a meaningful part of your story, and that it all really did happen for a reason.

As you travel on your long road to your heart's recovery, there will be times that it may not seem like you are progressing as much as you should be. Then one day, something will happen and things will become crystal clear. Suddenly you will know in your heart that you are whole again. You will feel free. You will understand that your relationship-and all the suffering you endured because of it- is really over. And when it is really over, it is *really over.*

Badda Bing, Badda Boom.

CPSIA information can be obtained
at www.ICGtesting.com
Printed in the USA
FFOW01n0623060115
9998FF